Endorsements by business leaders:

Facing a black swan event like the Covid pandemic, one needs a mindset and a toolbox that supports management in such an existential situation. MYPRISM provides such a toolbox on both accounts, providing very practical guidance and also giving fundamental advice. Nothing more and nothing less.

Tamur Goudarzi Pour, CCO, Swiss International Air Lines

MYPRISM is a practical book reflecting on a disillusioned Y-Generation of Executive Leaders. Why (the Y of MYPRISM) am I CEO, why and to what extent do I exercise the job as it is defined mainly by structures? More and more of my colleagues are asking these questions, and they are asked back the same questions. MYPRISM is the book that may help each of us to reflect on our REAL task and role, and to fundamentally change our leadership mindset and actions. MYPRISM offers a big tool set based on the experience of best-in-class coaches working in different cultures. MYPRISM can give orientation to find your way around today's need for out-of-the-box leadership. MYPRISM is well worth your time and an invitation to deep self-reflection.

Dr. Francesco De Meo, CEO Helios Health (#1 European healthcare group) and Member of the Management Board of Fresenius Management SE

Fascinating propositions for any leader who wants to lead in adverse times and ride the waves towards excellence. The book is a useful compendium as it clearly articulates how a leader can be deliberate in mindful thinking and move towards actions.

Ishak Ismail, Brigadier-General (Retired), Singapore Armed Forces, Former CEO, Consultant

The letters in MYPRISM say it all. M stands for Mindfulness. That is where it starts. In times like these with so many shifts of paradigms, when, if not now, should leaders take a breath and reflect on Why (Y), Perspectives (P) and Reality (R)? When, if not

now, should leaders strive for broader horizons and Inquire (I) and Stage (S) next steps before they Move (M)? This book answers many of the currently relevant questions leaders ask themselves or should ask themselves. Read it and find out!

CW, CEO - family holding and investment company

Good leadership does not happen by accident. MYPRISM makes this very clear. It is not only a unique acronym but also a thoughtful way of approaching the art of leadership (...) Based on real science, deliberate analysis, and informed insights, MYPRISM grounds the reader while driving home the point that good leadership is not automatic, accidental, or unconscious. Rather, it is well considered and based in fact, analysis, and a desire for constant improvement.

Rick Arai, Managing Director, Deloitte Global Technology Shared Services, Deloitte Services LP

MYPRISM offers a unique and practical guide for leaders to coach others -and themselves- in concrete, easy-to-follow steps. (...) [It] is also an engaging reading and a practical tool for self-learning, a must-read for leaders, mentors, teachers, and consultants.

Mariano Bernardez, PhD., CPT, CEO, Founder and Executive Director of the Performance Improvement Institute

MYPRISM is a book written by 6 coaches, coming from very different backgrounds. It is based on a scientific approach and experience with thousands of leaders. It will give you the opportunity to learn how to develop mindful leadership in a very concrete manner. You could use it in your professional life but also to lead your personal life with purpose.

Marie-Françoise Damesin, Board member and Senior Advisor, former CHRO

Sometimes we need to go a step back to move forward. MYPRISM is the perfect reminder on how important it is to listen, question the matter of course, reflect – and finally make better decisions moving forward. In a world that seems to become more dynamic and volatile day after day it is crucial to have a reliable compass. Who could offer this better than experienced coaches from different countries with different backgrounds and perspectives like the authors of MYPRISM?

Birgit Dengel, Director Corporate Communications & Public Relations, o2 Telefónica Germany; Expert for Positioning and Strategic Communications

Finally, a non-dogmatic book backed by science, written to help leaders discover and learn how to be their more effective, efficient, and impactful future selves. MYPRISM is such a book. (...) [T]he context for absorbing the contents of this book starts with the concept of autopilot that all of us necessarily develop. All of us have a very well-developed set of habits and routines that helps us meet the demands of our day. (...) However, between stimulus and response, there is space to pause. MYPRISM methodically guides the reader on how to use that space so that you don't default to your autopilot all the time and thus are likely to reach a more mindful, purposeful response. (...) MYPRISM is a frame of mind that cannot be switched on only when there is a crisis; it is a set of leadership practices: a repeatable methodology to ensure preparedness, confidence, and clarity for continued forward momentum.

Gary S. Farb, BA, JD, LLM (ADR)

With the intention of being a book at the service of leaders in their eternal process of evolution, it is an invitation to the self-development of our human consciousness. The 7 Facets of MYPRISM present a coherent and instructive approach for all those who directly or indirectly work with people.

José Augusto Figueiredo, The Adecco Group Country Head Brazil, Country Head Brazil & VP LHH AGG Latin America

I think especially now, when we are all experiencing 'chaos' on a weekly if not daily basis, the idea of pausing to reflect and reframe is so powerful. This framework provides a great structure for breaking down the steps and really immersing oneself in the pausing phase.

Jen F, Global L&D Senior Director, leading global consulting firm

The authors of MYPRISM provide a new perspective on leadership; however, I found the book went way beyond giving me a new model. I experienced it as revitalizing and invigorating. While reading it, I found myself reflecting on how I can embrace the ideas. I could imagine behaving in new ways, hearing more than what is shared, being open to new ideas, and taking the time to think differently. MYPRISM will be my "go to" resource for a long time.

Judith A. Hale, PhD, CPT, AIM. Author of nine books on consulting, measurement, and credentialing

MYPRISM is a perfect guide for leaders' own reflection. Scientific findings and decades of expertise of six renowned coaches worldwide offer condensed new aspects and helpful approaches to cut the invisible threads that often guide our actions: A valuable mindset for a more effective and impactful self and mindful leadership. Very well done.

Ilka Hartmann, Managing Director of the British Chamber of Commerce in Germany and Initiator of SHeconomy, Female Leaders Format

MYPRISM is a practical, insightful roadmap for personal, professional, and organizational transformation that combines outstanding academic research with real-world leadership coaching experience. It offers a very useful and easily accessible framework for current and aspiring leaders and, frankly, anyone who wishes to lead a more fulfilling and productive life personally or professionally. It highlights how one can be their best self through learned mindfulness, thoughtfulness, curiosity, courage, and openness. Curiosity may have killed the cat, but it created the leader!

Paul Kinscherff, Former President, The Boeing Company Middle East

This book is something I have been waiting for for a very long time. It promises to close a gap that many practitioners have been struggling with: if I know all the theories, if I am aware of the consequences of my actions, then where can I spot in my inner self when things are about to go "wrong", moving into autopilot even though I know and can do things so much better. Six highly qualified experts sensed this important gap and what they came up with, based on their global experience, is truly fascinating.

Dr. Matthias Lichtblau, Partner, Managing Director, Global Chief Operating Officer, WTS Global

Almost all managers are busy. Some of them are even "firefighters" of company crises – on a frequent basis. The reason is there is no mechanism that figures out "why we do what we do". MYPRISM offers a reliable answer of what a manager should do – not what a manager feels or likes to do. MYPRISM looks simple, but it is a result of years of collective thinking and practice.

George Limin Gu (顾立民), Co-founder, Improvement Consulting (改进咨询), Shanghai, CHINA, President-elect, International Society for Performance Improvement (ISPI)

Thoughtful. Provocative. Inspiring. If you want to lead more effectively and efficiently in a VUCA world, MYPRISM is the solution. You will learn a methodology that identifies and cultivates validated ways to turn off your autopilot reactions, build a more impactful self, and set yourself up for success to build the team's commitment to excellence.

Daniela Robu, MSc, CPT, CRP, CHE, Director I Innovation and Business Intelligence, Alberta Health Services, Calgary, Alberta, CANADA

To a steady drumbeat of self-leadership, the Kantologos offer us a sextet of practical advice. Their combined expertise and perspectives on what it takes to lead others well in times of change is rooted soundly in purpose and values. The Song of Logic, indeed.

Joe Slatter, Founder and CEO, Better Practice

Deep self-awareness can be seen as the essential ingredient of great leadership. MYPRISM is a precious tool to support any leader on this exciting lifelong learning journey of self-discovery and mindfulness.

Dr. Sven Sommerlatte, CHRO, Boehringer Ingelheim

Structure and logic, operational effectiveness and strong dedication have dominated our path and led many leaders to successful outcomes. In an ever-changing world where leaders face constantly evolving priorities, steaming ahead in one linear reality will no longer be successful nor viable. This insightful book will inspire many to take a conscious PRISM focus and, as mindful leaders, to take a breath and change perspectives before leaping ahead which will help them excel in leading themselves and others.

Sabine Weinheimer-Hoepermans, Global HRVP, CGI

More than ever, leaders and businesses must adapt to change, and this book offers a viable framework for all to adopt.

Galen Yeo, CEO, The Moving Visuals Co. Singapore

Endorsements by coaches:

As a biologist and coach interested in the intersection of leadership and well-being, MYPRISM is invaluable. It describes a way to lead your own neuroplasticity in the direction of a flexible and ever-changing prism, generating more complex neural networks, higher levels of consciousness, and continually expanding mindsets.

Margaret Moore, MBA; Founder/CEO, Wellcoaches Corporation; Co-Founder/Chair, Institute of Coaching, McLean Hospital, Harvard Medical School affiliate

Bravo to Kantologos! This book is a must-read! I have the privilege of calling the writers of this book, all senior executive coaches, and fellows with the IOC, both friend and colleague. They are seasoned coaches, brilliant minds, and deep thinkers about what leadership is called for in this world in serious transition. The themes in this book, and the tools and reflections are spot on. The MYPRISM framework provides depth and clarity and rich science underpinnings. I will be putting this work to use immediately with my clients -- and I'm so grateful that they took up the gauntlet to bring the fruits of their deep dialogue into the world in this accessible and highly readable format!

Jeffrey W. Hull, Ph.D., BCC; Executive Director, Institute of Coaching - McLean Hospital, a Harvard Medical School Affiliate; Clinical Instructor of Psychology, Harvard Medical School; CEO, LeaderShift, Inc.

If you are looking for an easy-to-apply and well-researched book on bringing forth your best self and discovering a new way of 'Being AND Becoming' – MYPRISM is it! For busy leaders and coaches who are interested in the applied aspect of the science and the art, particularly useful features are the thought-provoking questions and key takeaways in each chapter. (...) Like a masterly symphony, the story of designing for and implementing excellence with a sense of purpose comes alive in great harmony. This book is the perfect companion for anyone or any team which is interested in successfully surfing the waves of the chaotic yet opportunity-laden times we live in.

Jaspal Bajwa, MBA, PCC – Founder, 'Sunya Circle' - Coach & Consultant for Transformational Leadership & Organizational Vitality. Formerly, CXO & Profit-Center Head in leading global corporations.

As a neuroscience coach, focused on the awareness of the 'human being' vs. the 'human doing', I am delighted with the MYPRISM framework that encourages leaders to become aware of their learned behaviours that create their autopilot, and gives them a structure to help them stop for a moment and consider how leading on 'cruise control' is serving them, and if not, how to work towards change. The process of 'being' first, with mindfulness, asking why from a place of curiosity and exploring different perspectives, to a place of 'doing', when action after the reflection integrates the wisdom learned, is a pragmatic process to finding new ways of leading.

Hetty Brand-Boswijk, PCC, CNTC, ACTC, Director of Coaching/ Lead Coach, Rotterdam School of Management, Erasmus University Rotterdam

This is an exceptional book that showcases the collective experiences of six Fellows of the Institute of Coaching (IOC) who have all contributed their unique perspectives. The authors provide an insightful and practical guide to develop crucial leadership skills that are essential for navigating the challenges of a constantly changing world. The book presents a framework for leaders to manage their teams effectively. With exercises and cognitive interventions, readers can develop their self-regulation skills and make decisions that align with their values and purpose. Overall, this book is highly recommended for anyone looking to develop their leadership skills in a VUCA world.

Dr. Ruby Campbell, MSc, MBA, PhD, Managing Director, ProVeritas Leadership, Author of "Scientists in Every Boardroom: Harnessing the Power of STEMM Leaders in an Irrational World"

"Inspire, then Decide". This key idea resonates with me! The idea of resisting autopilot and choosing mindful leadership is a critical one, and MYPRISM provides practical tools and principles for achieving this goal. What sets MYPRISM apart is its focus on the relationship between leaders and their more effective and impactful future selves. MYPRISM is a must-read for any leader looking to enhance their preparedness and agility, and I highly recommend it to anyone seeking to become a more mindful and purposeful leader.

Fernando Celis, PCC ICF, Master Life Coach Trainer / Master Coach IAC, CEO and Founder ILC Academy

Increasing our capacity to continuously make and implement difficult decisions for ourselves, our loved ones, colleagues, employees, and customers is one of the greatest challenges of our time. And it is exhausting! The Kantologos author team, deeply experienced coaches and leadership experts, has synthesized more than 100 years of coaching experience with hundreds of books, articles and research studies to create the MYPRISM approach to problem solving. This book lays out the how, why, and what of effective problem solving. A must read for all leaders and coaches.

Edy Greenblatt, PhD, #1 Global Resilience Coach, Award-winning Author, "Restore Yourself: The Antidote for Professional Exhaustion", Creator of the Resilience Oasis App

MYPRISM is a powerful framework that helps leaders not only take their skills to the next level, but also develop a more impactful future self. Written by real coaching practitioners, the book offers a collection of unique insights. It comes at just the right time because mindful leadership is needed today more than ever.

Christian Greiser, C-Suite Coach, Strategist and Author, Senior Advisor and Senior Partner Emeritus Boston Consulting Group

MYPRISM outlines a methodology that is a great tool for leaders to build a more conscious and intentional approach to stressful situations. (...) The emphasis on cultivating mindfulness and self-awareness is especially notable. Leaders may develop a deeper knowledge of their mission and ideals by fostering these vital traits, which will allow them to respond more calmly and effectively to any difficult scenario. (...) Overall, I strongly suggest this book to anybody who wants to become a more successful, efficient, and influential version of themselves, particularly leaders who want to become more attentive and deliberate in their responses to difficult situations.

Donna Karlin, CEO and Founder of the No Ceiling Just Sky™ Institute.

MYPRISM is a vital resource for mindful and resilient leadership. It integrates scientific evidence with practical tools, to activate the "creative and curious brain" that may be asleep on "autopilot". After all, "who we are determines how we lead", so MYPRISM is a must read to be and do "better" at the personal and professional level.

Sule Kutlay Gandur, Leadership Coach & Consultant, TEDx Speaker, Certified Forum Facilitator for YPO, Fellow at IOC McLean Harvard

MYPRISM is convincing in its clarity and comprehensibility, how I can improve as a leader in my decision-making and implementation process. Viktor Frankl once said that between stimulus and reaction lies a space. In this space lies our power to choose our reaction. In our reaction lies our development and our freedom. These 6 experienced and international coaches show us scientific methods, concepts, and practical examples to achieve this freedom in a purposeful and well-guided way.

Lars Maydell, Executive Coach and Business Adviser to CEOs, Industry Advisory Board Member of CoachHub, the digital coaching platform

Any external change depends on an internal change. Especially when we want to promote effective and lasting change. MYPRISM brings clarity to the process. It helps leaders to broaden their perspectives, question their truths and adopt different attitudes to produce different results. MYPRISM is an interesting path to facilitate this process, created by a brilliant international group of coaches who combined deep knowledge of leadership and solid experience in human development. This book is a valuable contribution for those who want to become better leaders and agents of transformation!

Silvia Micelli, Mentor and transformational Coach, Founder of UNO Performance Integral

MYPRISM is a new space opening up at a perfect time. (...) We need to upgrade our thinking and decision-making framework to, literally, stay alive and possibly thrive. MYPRISM gifts us "the how" - to pilot our own and our followers' lives. Autopilot is a function - an algorithm; Pilot is a Human. (...) To decide fast a Pilot needs a pre-wired mental framework, a decision-making path to deploy her intelligence in time. MYPRISM is the fast-response framework for a Pilot - for me, for you. (...) [It] enlightens the path, pioneered by the authors, to move from Important to Relevant, Anxious to Creative, Stimulus to Response for becoming a better leader. (...) I admire and deeply respect each of the authors and recommend this intellectual and developmental journey for the better future for all of us.

Rafał Milek-Horodyski MD, EMBA, HORODYSKI Leadership Development International

In MYPRISM, the authors introduce a powerful framework for leaders to discover new opportunities beyond the constraints of their habitual thinking and behaviours. Profound, science-based concepts are translated into a hands-on, step-by-step guide on how to integrate new perspectives into leadership practices. This book captures the keys to enhance clarity, decision-making, and performance while building authenticity. I could immediately apply what I learned from MYPRISM in my own work with clients in different countries and industries.

Juan Pablo Ortiz, Partner and Senior Management Consultant. YesP Consulting, Sweden

This valuable book, based on scientific research findings as well as real-life experience from experts in the field, will equip you to leave your default "autopilot" mode and engage instead on a fulfilling, exciting and purposeful life journey.

Prof. Philippe Rosinski, Master Certified Coach, Author of "Coaching Across Cultures" and "Global Coaching"

This book represents the collective wisdom six experienced master coaches have harvested from coaching thousands of clients in countries around the world, now synthesized into an accessible volume. Leaders and aspiring leaders who wish to develop and leverage nuanced awareness of the situations around them and their own patterns of thinking and behaviour will gain increased agility and effectiveness by learning the concepts and practicing the thoughtful exercises presented in this book. It's a valuable reference and guide for anyone who wants to work and live with intention and impact.

Monique Valcour, PhD PCC, Executive Coach · Learning Catalyst

As an executive coach, I see, as do the authors, that mindfulness is the #1 leadership skill of today. In MYPRISM, their global perspective brings new aspects to integrating mindfulness into leadership that translate very well to different cultures and work settings. The book is a practical guide for leaders and coaches alike to become aware of their autopilot in daily actions and to find ways to be more conscious and better with themselves and others. The neuroscientific underpinnings convince even sceptics that we need mindfulness skills for leadership in order to continue to be successful. A book worth reading that I strongly recommend to every leader and coach.

Brigitta Wurnig, Top Management Coach, Hamburg, Author of "On the Way-Experiences with Digital Leadership"

Endorsements by education leaders:

The authors succeed in compiling a unique and highly useful book for today's busy leaders. Leaders are learners and this book endows them with a holistic framework to become even better.

Wolfgang Amann, Professor of Strategy and Leadership, HEC Paris in Qatar

Six thoughtful risk takers from five different countries have collaborated in a setting, the Institute of Coaching (IOC), that has often produced a Medici effect in the field of coaching. These expert coaches are addressing the challenges of VUCA (to which I would add turbulence and contradiction). I love their use of metaphor (prism can see around obstacles) and their deployment of an organizing acronym (MYPRISM) (each letter representing a rich concept). I also appreciate the foundation they have established with mindfulness (M). I will be re-reading their book many times and incorporating their concepts in my own work and writing.

William Bergquist, Ph.D, author of more than 50 books, co-curator of the digital Library of Professional Coaching and curator of the digital Library of Professional Psychology.

MYPRISM is a brilliant addition to leadership literature. The authors' five-country breadth of experience gives the reader a useful perspective on the commonality of leadership dilemmas, and practical applications for what to do. "Key take-aways" summarize the high points in chapters. Case studies offer opportunities for reflection. This is a practical book and will be a reference you will return to again and again.

Margaret Cary, MD MBA MPH PCC

MYPRISM unpacks the steps and skills of effectively engaging with a changing world by going beyond our autopilot responses, so relevant for our current world of chaos and crisis. I'm not usually a fan of acronyms, but this book's name strikes me as powerful in itself to remind us we see the world through our "prisms." It also unpacks each element with full doses of body awareness, emotions, choices, and actions. From Mindfulness to Move each step is empowering. Kudos to the authors (...) This book is going to be one of my companions.

Bob Dunham, Founder of the Institute for Generative Leadership. Co-author of "The Power of Owning Up" (with Sameer Dua) and "The Innovator's Way" (with Peter Denning)

Executives in marketing, sales and other business functions will benefit greatly from the holistic perspective provided by the seven facets of MYPRISM. In moments of high stress and beyond, the wisdom offered in this book will help leaders sustain performance, ensure employee well-being, and avoid negative effects of autopilot.

Frank Q. Fu, Ph.D., Associate Professor of Marketing, University of Missouri - St. Louis

MYPRISM combines strong scientific research, powerful examples, easy to remember mnemonics, sound guidance, and helpful exercises to integrate its lessons into a reader's life. It is a guide towards living more consciously, becoming more self-aware, taking ownership of the opportunities that life presents, and taking responsibility for the responses we choose, all in service of living our best life. (...) MYPRISM provides sound advice for creating a life of meaning and integrity, lessons we can all grow from.

Rabbi Sidney M. Helbraun, Temple Beth-El

MYPRISM was written in service of the relationship between leaders and their more effective capacity to lead. Few leadership books are as comprehensive and detailed as MYPRISM, truly a global team effort. No book on leadership is more globally relevant than MYPRISM, authored by six coaches from five countries on four continents. (...) [It] is indispensable for leaders and coaches alike – and, increasingly, leaders identify as coaches to their people, making this book a must-read. MYPRISM is a practical book, incorporating not only thoughtfulness, but that movement and action that all leadership requires. This book is a huge contribution to the leader development field.

Tom Kolditz, PhD, Brigadier General, US Army (ret), Founding Director, Ann & John Doerr Institute for New Leaders, Rice University, Professor Emeritus, US Military Academy, West Point, Author of "In Extremis Leadership: Leading as if Your Life Depended On It" and "Leadership Reckoning: Can Higher Education Develop the Leaders we Need?"

The title MYPRISM intuitively reminded of the interplay of light and colours that create patterns and reflection. The international team of experienced executive coaches present a powerful methodology for modern leaders in highly interconnected and pluralistic societies, where inspiring leadership is a differentiator – equipped with tools how to reflect, reframe, and repower their spaces with clarity and purpose.

Jozefina Kontic, Business Development Director DACH at Headspring Executive Development

I am happy to see this international group of experienced coaches put their heads together and distil key learning points from their work with thousands of leaders. Take advantage of this condensed knowledge for your own development and for supporting others.

Konstantin Korotov, Professor of Organizational Behavior, ESMT Berlin

The MYPRISM model is attractive, positive, stimulating, and full of fresh ideas. It offers effective and practical means to augment understanding of both internal and external forces that threaten to undermine the courage, confidence, and clarity needed to grow and lead. MYPRISM could be identified as a field guide for coaching during times of uncertainty; it provides a model and guidance for how to get re-centered and well prepared to face the myriad of problems emerging in our personal and professional lives. Now instead of just wringing our hands at the obvious plethora of functional problems bequeathed to us during these disruptive times, this group of professionals provide insights into how to address our individual and collective challenges in a unique and effective way.

Karl E. Scheibe, Ph.D, Professor of Psychology Emeritus, Wesleyan University, Middletown, CT

It's hard to make good leadership decisions in times of crisis, when the autopilot that leaders typically use to get through their working days becomes useless and even counterproductive. To help leaders build and hone skills to override their autopilots, the Kantologos have created the MYPRISM framework. Leaders lead themselves and their teams by being mindful, asking why, exploring multiple perspectives, determining what is really happening, inquiring, staging, and moving. To make the framework clear and approachable, the authors provide multiple Illustrative case studies drawn from their real-world experiences. (...) I fully endorse this insightful and helpful text!

Steven W. Villachica, PhD, Emeritus Professor, Organizational Performance and Workplace Learning (OPWL), Boise State University

While living in a chaotic world where machines seem to take over our lives and the lives of our organizations, each leader has the responsibility to clarify and define their own purpose and the best way to create a better future. From my personal point of view, MYPRISM is a methodology introduced by prestigious coaches that utilizes their science-based knowledge and experience to help leaders intentionally apply mindful leadership to be more effective and have a better impact developing themselves. I strongly recommend reading and understanding their framework.

Gonzalo Rodriguez Villanueva, PhD, Past President of the Sonora Technological Institute (ITSON), Professor of Economics, recipient of the Kaufman Award for social impact given by the International Society for Performance Improvement, Director of the Regional Center of Innovation in Sonora, Mexico.

When I read MYPRISM I was reminded of the question, "How do you eat an elephant?" The answer: "one bite at a time." MYPRISM is an articulate, well-organized, and practical primer for mindful, purposeful leadership in our chaotic, messy, and uncertain world. Grounded in science and salient data, contextualized with effective real-world, illustrative vignettes, MYPRISM cumulatively builds as it works to help the reader increase their own capacities for a mindfulness practice to become the agent of their own leadership transformation, to empower others as they strengthen their respective organizations, and to ultimately have even more effective, far-reaching impact. (...) Here's to embracing the prism metaphor. May it include more than a nod to the late Rev. Dr. Martin Luther King, Jr.'s wise words, "the arc of the moral universe is long, but it bends toward justice." That will only be possible with the collective action of an enlightened leadership body which is that much more likely in part due to the release of this book.

Wendy Sternberg, MD, Founder and Executive/Artistic Director, Genesis at the Crossroads, Physician Consultant and Public Health Strategist

MYPRISM
Override Your Autopilot
Choose Mindful Leadership

Maribel Aleman, Douglas Choo,
John Lazar, Beth Masterman,
Fernando Morais and Rolf Pfeiffer

KANTOLOGOS

PERSPECTIVES + POSSIBILITIES

CHANGING THE WAY WE THINK

First edition published in the United Kingdom in 2023 by Ideas for Leaders Publishing, a business of IEDP Ideas for Leaders Ltd.

Ideas for Leaders Publishing
42 Moray Place
Edinburgh
EH3 6BT
www.ideasforleaders.com
info@ideasforleaders.com

ISBNs
978-1-915529-14-5 – Paperback
978-1-915529-15-2 – Hardback
978-1-915529-11-4 – Ebook

Cover design: www.nickmortimer.co.uk
Typesetting: Sopho Tarkashvili

With immense gratitude to our families, friends, clients, colleagues, and mentors who inspired and supported us to write MYPRISM

Contents

Foreword xxv
Carol Kauffman

Chapter 1 3
Introduction

Chapter 2 17
'M' is for Mindfulness

Chapter 3 41
'Y' is for Why

Chapter 4 63
'P' is for Perspective

Chapter 5 87
'R' is for Reality

Chapter 6 109
'I' is for Inquiry

Chapter 7 131
'S' is for Staging

Chapter 8 147
'M' is for Move

Chapter 9 159
Case Study and Exercise

Epilogue 169

Notes 175

Bibliography 187

Index 197

Foreword

As the founder and co-chair of the Institute of Coaching at McLean, a Harvard Medical School Affiliate, I cannot be prouder of the Kantologos, an outstanding group of self-selected Fellows for coming together to produce this book. At the Institute it is our goal to mentor as many coaches as possible to maintain and elevate the standard of coaching. This group, with their book MYPRISM, provides an excellent example of our efforts. They are a worthy testimony to our commitment to the dissemination of evidence-based coaching leavened with great experience to help create best practices. I congratulate the team!

It was the first official week of COVID lockdown when our world was suddenly tilted off its axis. Like many practices that are now common I quickly organized and hosted what we called "huddles." These online group meetings were offered to the Fellows at the Institute of Coaching. With the world locked down in isolation, self-care and connection became more central to our lives. I felt it important to generate even higher levels of engagement amongst the Fellows as bastions of the coaching profession. In so doing they could continue to be of optimal service to their client leaders during such difficult times. To give an idea of the scope of influence IOC coaches make, our clients include leaders of multibillion dollar global organizations, or are heads of major non-profits, founders or high potentials, so our Leadership coaching fellows have direct and indirect impact on tens of millions of managers and workers.

Fellows responded immediately gathering at least twice a week at times that could accommodate our entire global community. The meetings evolved from sharing experiences to group supervision to collective thought-leadership.

Fellows started presenting ideas for articles on the theory and practice of coaching. We were now energizing and galvanizing thought-leadership in executive coaching.

During their meetings the Kantologos challenged one another on their coaching approaches, pushed their learning and encouraged mutual coaching supervision. The work shared here is the result of one year of weekly meetings where they would come up with challenging issues to hone each other's coaching skills and learning. During that process, Maribel, Douglas, John, Beth, Fernando, and Rolf, came to the fore and published their first joint article on "Resilience" on LinkedIn.

With that article, the group pushed further along the way, I planted the idea of a book as an appropriate culmination of their work. "Why not amplify your impact as coaches with a book that many can access? What good is good thinking not shared?", I challenged. Quietly, and with conviction, they continued their collaboration, and the result is "MYPRISM" which is the acronym for

M is for Mindfulness which is the integration of awareness, focus, practice and reflection;

Y is the onomatopoeia for "why" which explores the cognitive science of human motivation; why we behave the way we do;

P is for perspective taking;

R is for a reality check;

I is for investigate, integrate and inspire

S is for staging

M is for moving with all the above in operation

Collectively, the six authors have over 100 years of coaching experience. 100 years! Very few books can claim to embody such a wealth of experience. Each chapter draws on their actual coaching experience, and while the descriptions of the coaching are accurate the leaders have been disguised, out of respect for their privacy. The case studies are poignant lessons for coaches and the coached alike. What might we all learn from these cases?

MYPRISM is about overriding our autopilot, avoiding our blind spots and commitment to always be guided by our deeper purpose in the behavioral choices we make. I hope you love the metaphor the Kantologos have created of the prism, which draws on concepts from physics to aptly depict the complexity of behavioural science. With the prism, you can split a beam of light into its segments and then with another one at the other end, redirect that same beam towards a more purposeful outcome. With two prisms, you can literally bend light and see round the corner. Brilliant idea! Simple, but so complex in its execution. That is why this book is so powerful. If you spend time with it, and I encourage you to read it over-and-over again, you will uncover many layers of cognitive abilities that you can practise, hone and master. Do not avoid the exercises in each chapter. These are cleverly designed to tone your self-regulation muscles.

Although MYPRISM was borne from the volatile, uncertain, complex and ambiguous days of a pandemic, I believe it is relevant for all times. Laid out in an easy-to-follow sequence from internal mindfulness to execution, it invites you to embark on a journey of self-learning. It does not impose. It maintains a very Socratic approach – the very foundation of effective coaching. It makes you reflect and come to your own conclusions. It is like having a member of the Kantologos in the room with you, coaching you. I am very confident you will enjoy this journey.

Congratulations Maribel, Douglas, John, Beth, Fernando, and Rolf! Well done. Most of all, to all the readers of MYPRISM congratulations also to you for picking up this book. You have taken a very important first step towards self-discovery and self-betterment.

Carol Kauffman

Founder of the Institute of Coaching

(IOC, Harvard Medical School Affiliate)

March, 2023

MYPRISM

Override Your Autopilot Choose Mindful Leadership

Maribel Aleman, Douglas Choo,
John Lazar, Beth Masterman,
Fernando Morais and Rolf Pfeiffer

CHAPTER 1

Introduction

In the early days of the 2020 COVID-19 Pandemic, as the world suffered self-isolation and endured lockdowns, Professor Carol Kauffman, Founder of the Institute of Coaching (IOC, Harvard Medical School Affiliate) started weekly virtual huddles amongst Fellows of the IOC. These huddles served as a forum for leading executive coaches around the world to stay connected and share observations and ideas on how leaders were responding to the crisis. This book is inspired by Professor Kauffman.

What emerged from the IOC huddles were deep discussions around resilience. From self care to corporate survival, leaders were unanimous on the need to focus on mental well-being and personal motivation in order to sustain individual and team performance. Prof. Kauffman challenged the group for fresh insights or approaches to coaching executives on building resilience – a fundamental leadership skill to handle the chaotic world we were living in at the time. We considered such questions as: Is there such a thing as too much resilience? What is the line between resilience and senseless endurance? How do we know if we crossed that line?

The six authors of this book (all Fellows of the IOC) decided to take on the challenge. Inspired by our colleagues at the IOC and Prof. Kauffman, we formed the group Kantologos. We called ourselves "The Kantologos" mainly because it was Prof. Carol Kauffman who brought us together via the Institute of Coaching. Carol is Latin for song. Esperanto for song is "Kanto". Logos is Greek for logic. Thus, we decided to call ourselves, "The Song of Logic".

We pulled our collective experiences and readings together to publish a compendium offering a fresh perspective on resilience, an important leadership skill that we argued can be developed and honed. The compendium also discussed the potential dark side of resilience. The compendium we published included three articles:

- "A Leader's Resilience: Not As Intuitive As You Think" by Douglas Choo, which highlighted the importance of self-awareness.
- "Resilience and Human Nature" by Beth Masterman and Fernando Morais, which expanded on self-awareness to find strength from our innate human nature and our environment.
- "Resilience Does Not Equal Great Leadership" by Maribel P. Aleman and John B. Lazar, which created a pathway for growth from three perspectives by looking inward, outward, and forward.

We were also invited by the American Association of Corporate Counsel to present our papers at their 2021 Annual General Meeting, where more than 100 members dialed in from around the world to listen to what we had to say. Encouraged by the success of our first collective effort, we set off to challenge ourselves to deepen our thinking and approach to leadership in our current volatile, uncertain, complex, and ambiguous (VUCA) world. (We discuss the VUCA complex in more detail later in this chapter.)

Based on our collective knowledge and experience from our respective coaching practices, we wanted to develop a framework to guide decision-making for leaders managing and directing teams facing the challenges of a volatile and changing world. When under stress, the human brain defaults to what it is most comfortable with, relying on historical lessons to navigate out of uncertainty. Defaulting to an "autopilot" reaction is efficient when there is no time to think and the world has not changed in significant ways. Action is needed. Inaction, which only leads to more uncertainty and reflects leadership weakness, must be avoided.

"Autopilot" is thus a natural default behaviour choice in the face of change, which is scary and uncertain. The human brain, wired to resist change, defaults to what has worked in the past. However, if left unchecked, "autopilot" can lead us into blind spots. It exaggerates our reality, clouds perspectives, and more often than not leads to suboptimal solutions.

We thus began asking ourselves: Is defaulting to autopilot the best solution? Might "autopilot" create more risks? Might there be a better way to respond than relying on "autopilot"? When do we decide? How would we know?

As we pondered these questions, we wondered if by understanding our internal cognitive process, we might learn how to intervene, self-regulate, and optimize our actions to achieve the desired purpose required by the external environment. We might learn how to organize our resources to best address crises, which will typically be evolving. We could develop a method that offers a natural way to deal with a crisis – one that is not dependent on historical experience but rather responds to changing internal and external conditions with fresh perspectives.

These are some of the issues this book will discuss. Understanding the science behind cognitive and behavioural choices is the first step towards learning skills for higher self-regulation and cognitive interventions, which ensures that every decision is grounded in values and purpose. In this book, we will share exercises on how this skill can be practiced and honed. Over time, the practices we offer will develop a new way of being.

Beyond crisis management

The COVID-19 pandemic, with its global, unexpected, disruptive, frightening, and challenging impact, affected us all significantly. The very first reactions from China to the rest of the world were "freeze" behaviours as there were no "fight" or "flight" alternatives envisaged – no one had a clear idea of what it was, let alone what to do. We witnessed the rush to stockpile food and supplies, as health guidelines on isolation and public gatherings followed a haphazard timeline and geographical reach.

Early in 2020, public health authorities and a growing number of epidemiologists began to share information on the behaviour of the virus and its movement from East to West; it became evident that some patterns were emerging and that some level of predictability about the spread of the disease was possible. Anxious, threatened, and confused, the world did not have the patience to wait for answers from leading experts and political leaders who were offering no clear answers.

The chaos of this unexpected and devastating situation, in which we did not even know what we did not know about this new virus, gave rise to many amateur epidemiologists and their followers who clung to quantitative models that purported to provide some level of predictability and certainty about the evolution of the terrifying pandemic. It was their way to cope, their way to find certainty and safety when in fact such certainty and safety did not exist. This illusion of certainty and safety, however, was better than not knowing, which for many people was not an acceptable condition.

This was a global crisis, and in response, crisis management kicked into high gear.

In support of this crisis management momentum, Harvard Business School in late March and early April 2020 provided the general public access to a series of classes on Crisis Management for Leaders and used the emerging pandemic as the subject of their reflection[1].

These classes yielded two key elements defined as vital to dealing with a crisis of COVID's magnitude:

Perspective: clarity not certainty

Governance: expand decision process governance

However, the impact and ramifications of COVID-19 had shown that traditional theories of crisis management were inefficient in dealing with the pandemic. A virus does not discriminate between management and staff. Theories of management have to be revisited and refined. Leaders need to reach a personal level, a humanistic approach to managing and motivating their people. This humanistic approach was indeed one of the topics covered in the IOC huddles hosted by Prof. Kauffman.

The Age of Chaos

The COVID-19 pandemic only compounded the increasingly difficult challenges for leaders to make sense and choose appropriate lines of conduct and action in the world we live in – a world characterized by Jamais Cascio (wikipedia), a leading futurist and Fellow of The Institute For The Future (IFTF), as "the age of chaos." In his article, "Facing the Age of Chaos", Cascio argues that:

"... This current moment of political mayhem, climate disasters, and global pandemic–and so much more– vividly demonstrates the need for a way of making sense of the world, the need for a new method or tool to see the shapes this age of chaos takes ... if we can make disruptive processes understandable, we hope, maybe we can keep their worst implications in check.... "[2]

One concept that captures the dynamics of change in this age of chaos is the "VUCA" concept. VUCA is an acronym for Volatile, Uncertain, Complex, and Ambiguous. The term "VUCA", which first appeared in the work of the US Army War College in the late 1980s, is a useful way to make some sense of an ever-changing world. If we characterize and recognize change as a function of one or many of these dynamics at play, we can develop the appropriate tools to address the change – although, as Cascio warns us,

> "... tools don't tell us what will happen, they (only) enable us to understand the parameters of what could happen in a volatile (uncertain, etc.) world. ...."

One of the most compelling tools created to handle VUCA challenges was developed by Robert Johansen, founder and Distinguished Fellow of the IFTF. Johansen, who spent decades devising and developing mechanisms to address our VUCA world (Johansen, 2007, 2009, 2020), created a meaningful set of principles that transform the VUCA acronym to serve as an antidote. He states that:

> "... Leaders in the future will need to have Vision, Understanding, Clarity, and Agility. The negative VUCA can be turned around with effective leadership that follows these principles:

- Volatility yields to Vision.
- Uncertainty yields to Understanding.

- Complexity yields to Clarity.

- Ambiguity yields to Agility.

As Johansen warns: "... the VUCA world of the future will be formidable and loaded with opportunities. The biggest danger is not being prepared – and you can control that by preparing yourself and your organization".

The complex challenges of our VUCA world have inspired us, the Kantologos, to draw on our collective experiences in coaching and business consulting to develop a toolset to help leaders navigate the stormy waters ahead. Our toolset is built on the metaphor of a Prism.

Why MYPRISM?

Refraction is the change in direction of a wave passing from one medium to another or from a gradual change in the medium. Refraction of light is the most commonly observed phenomenon, but other waves such as sound waves and water waves also experience refraction.

When light enters, exits, or changes at an angle the medium it travels in, one side of the wavefront is slowed before the other. This asymmetrical slowing of the light causes it to change the angle of its travel. The difference in medium also impacts the wavelength of light. This causes light to be dispersed into its constituent colours–hence the rainbow. The prism breaks light into its constituents; it also causes the light to change its direction. Putting two prisms next to each other can cause light to "bend" and go round a corner.

We found the metaphor of the prism compelling to describe the challenges of a leader who is facing unchartered waters. Indeed, the physics behind the working of the prism provides parallels to the cognitive science on which our leadership framework is built. Consider the physics of the prism:

- Refraction does not distort light. However, it has the ability to bend light, to change its angle without changing its constituents. How would leaders gain a broader perspective while working with the situation presenting itself? Rather than trying to control and change the situation to yield to their will, would leaders navigate through a medium successfully while not distorting reality?

- The effects of refraction depend on the medium through which light passes. The medium in our approach is the metaphor for culture, religion, political orientation, economic perspective, etc., and this leads to different perspectives. These "mediums" impact how a leader might see light.

- A prism unweaves the spectrum of light into its respective colour constituents. How might a leader break down and see the constituents that make up the reality of the situation – what is factual vs. perception vs. opinion? What is the reality confronting the team or the organization?

In the following chapters, we will describe our approach to leadership decision-making and provide an action plan. The overall objective is to avoid the dark side of autopilot, especially during moments of high stress and uncertainty. We coined our approach as "MYPRISM", with each letter representing an important step in our methodology. We believe practitioners of "MYPRISM" will be more masterful in self-regulation, increasing resilience, and developing and executing creative solutions especially when the going gets tough. It is our hope that readers of "MYPRISM" will develop a new approach to crises—one that is driven not by fear and anxiety but by purpose and creativity. And use this approach outside of crises, too.

In each chapter, we start with the description of a case based on our coaching experience. The identities of the clients are disguised and in some cases, we combined several individuals into one. This will ensure client privacy and remove any chance of any readers guessing the identities. We use the opening case to discuss the behavioural science behind the theory of our approach. Next, we demonstrate the working of the theory through the coaching we provided in each case. We then end each chapter with practical exercises to enable you to hone your cognitive skills.

We start with M for Mindfulness: In this chapter, we discuss how mindfulness is the core to purposeful decision-making and action. We expand on the practice of being acutely aware of your internal conditions as well as your external environment. We provide guidelines on how to focus your awareness by integrating sensations, feelings, emotions, and thoughts. With mindfulness, the anxious brain calms down much faster, which in turn enables the curious brain to step forward. With mindfulness, the VUCA world will become much more manageable and navigable. Mindfulness helps to avoid an autopilot approach – but it is not enough. We will provide, in this book, a structured approach to extend our mindfulness.

We move to Y which stands for Why: We begin this chapter with a discussion on how the human brain is naturally wired to need to know why. We cannot help ourselves. We cannot refrain from asking questions. This quest for knowledge and meaning is a survival instinct, a human instinct. Once we understand how our brain works, we explore how to hone and tap into this unique human instinct to propel us towards creativity rather than let it burden us with rumination, doubt, and anxiety. We look at questions such as: Why are you reacting to this vs. what is the performance demand of the moment? What is your original purpose and desired outcome? How would you satisfy your brain's need to know why, and find the motivation you need and move towards creativity? We provide drills to help you with this.

P is for Perspective, for choosing Point(s) of View: There are multiple experiments and anecdotes that demonstrate that the same exact picture conveys different meanings and invites different conclusions from different viewers. If we are able to open our aperture, stand at a distance for a systems-wide view, might we see things that we previously missed? Might we change our assumptions or biases? Might our behavioural choices change as a result? How do we even know that we have blind spots, let alone take steps to avoid them? In this chapter, we explore these and other questions that challenge you to broaden your perspective. As with the other chapters, we end this chapter with a set of practical exercises that you can do on your own to expand your intake of data and your perspective.

R is for Reality: Now that you've acquired an expanded perspective, this chapter helps you see "reality" for what it is rather than through only one set of eyes (yours). We discuss how you can avoid distortions based on historical experience and conscious and/or unconscious biases. You will also learn how to identify a fact vs. an assumption. Your reality is based on both observable data and unobservable data. Being aware that the context of your situation is also shaped by the reality perceived by others, you will be better positioned to choose a path forward that is based on all aspects of your reality vs. just what your brain tells you to see.

I is for Investigate, Integrate, Inspire: You may ask, "So what is 'REALITY'?" Is everything then a matter of perspective and context? In this chapter, we demonstrate the power of inquiry. If you start every stressful moment with a curious mind, you will find that your autopilot, which is switched to "anxiety" mode, can be flipped to the "off" position. With your autopilot switched off, your new stance is now probing for data, intel, and solutions. Teaching you how to integrate all that you have investigated and how to use this new insight to inspire is an important part of our methodology. You will also learn how to unleash your creativity by asking that one more question even when you think you know the answer. This will avoid the blind spots that come with an unchecked autopilot.

S is for Staging: Now that you are mindfully aware of your internal and external conditions, you are clear about your purpose and are able to collate vast data with an inquiring mind. You also see things from a wider and different angle. Your reality is now "holistic". You are ready to act. But not so fast. Our methodology is about creating a space between a trigger and a reaction so that each step you take is a purposeful response. Hence, we introduce "STAGING". Staging is the process of actively designing how we engage, execute, and exit once the decision has been made. It is about proactively orchestrating your resources to move in sync to reach your goal. At its very core, staging is about planning and orchestrating a masterful execution.

Finally, M stands for Move: In this chapter, we focus on action. By action, we also include internal activation as much as outward behaviour. This chapter is about taking steps mentally and physically to effect the change that you have mindfully designed and staged. Without "MOVE", all you have achieved is insight without transformation. Transformation is hard because we are naturally wired to resist change. Change requires courage and effort. Our default is to repeat what we know because familiarity is comforting. Hence, the autopilot. We invite you to turn off your autopilot. As with the other chapters, we include practical steps that you can take to effect the change you want.

We conclude this book the way we started: with a case study. This final case study illustrates MYPRISM in action. Autopilot is clearly inadequate to handle a VUCA world. MYPRISM is our contribution to help leaders, indeed anyone, to get out of autopilot and purposefully navigate the VUCA world. We wanted to create something that was easy to understand although founded on comprehensive and well-researched science of human behaviour. You can choose to remember only the acronym by scanning this chapter or pick the chapter that best reflects your current and most urgent query, or you can choose to read this book cover to cover. Any way you choose to read this book, we have written it so you can heighten your senses and sharpen your actions as you navigate the situation/world you live in.

Although borne out of the COVID-19 pandemic crisis, we believe the approach described in this book is timeless and applicable to leading and managing our changing world in general. We hope it will help our readers discover and hone their cognitive skills to extend their leadership range so that every leader has an autopilot that is mindful, purposeful, and adaptable over time, rather than merely an emotional reaction based on historical experiences.

CHAPTER 2

"M" is for Mindfulness

I feel newborn with every moment
To the complete newness of the world...
Fernando Pessoa[1]

Mindfulness in Practice: Awareness, Focus, Practice, Reflection

Overview

As discussed in Chapter 1, developing a set of skills and a process to avoid our autopilot is essential to managing the challenges of a VUCA world. Since autopilot is learned behaviour based on historical experiences, we must have a better understanding of our internal cognitive processes in order to increase our capabilities to self-regulate, intervene, and optimize our actions in ever-changing and challenging times. Based on this knowledge, we can integrate and regulate sensations, feelings, emotions, and thoughts, leading to more positive and effective behaviours and decision-making processes.

In this chapter we will develop a working definition of what mindfulness is and present a practical approach to increase our self-awareness and focus, prepare for purposeful decision making and action, and reflect on this experience so that the learnings can expand our cognitive skills beyond our autopilot.

Case Study: Unaware, Unfocused and Unprepared

Florence was a partner at a strategy consulting boutique. She had arrived for the meeting at the client's site early that morning after a short 45-minute flight. As they shuttled from the airport, she talked only very briefly to the driver for she wanted to use that half-hour drive to review the meeting's agenda and to browse through her email.

This would be the third of a series of meetings to evaluate and discuss a proposal for a merger presented by the client's larger and more powerful competitor. The meeting went quite well. She facilitated a discussion with the client's senior leadership team and a consensus was obtained about the company's positioning and counter proposal related to key aspects of the merger.

At 5 pm that day, she was on the road again, going back to the airport to take another flight that would take her directly to the city where, the next morning, she would have a project review meeting at another client's location. After years of leading this intense consulting life, Florence had developed an "expertise" in high-efficiency, high-quality traveling experiences and this trip was an excellent example of how far she had progressed.

Because of her efficiency, she would not have to wake up at 4 am as she used to. Instead, she would be able to sleep a little longer and then go for a 45-minute power-walk on the wooden deck along the beach, enjoying the sea breeze and listening to one of her favourite business podcasts. She would then have a reinvigorating shower and enjoy that wonderful, light, tropical fruit breakfast – what a treat!

Enjoying the view from her room, the business day would begin with a quick browse at her email and a calm review of a preliminary project status report, the core of that morning's meeting agenda: some cost-overrun issues had been detected and she needed some extra time to evaluate the situation carefully...

Halfway to the airport, there she was, immersed in her thoughts about what the next day would bring when suddenly she looked outside and noticed that, surprisingly, the sky was getting cloudy and dark. Thunder and lightning were becoming more frequent. It looked like one of those typical tropical storms was fast rolling in. Noticing her surprise, the driver told her that the storm would probably hit them earlier than forecasted. A couple of miles later, the first large raindrops splashed on the windscreen, and in less than ten minutes they felt blindfolded by the grey curtain that made the windscreen wipers useless. Wind gusts, thunder, and lightning were getting more and more intense. The driver was bending forward over the wheel, trying to guess what the next visible thirty yards would reserve for them.

"In my 20 years as a driver in this area, madam, I have never seen anything like this! I am worried... I think that we would better stop at the rest area that is a few minutes ahead and wait for the storm to pass, madam!"

"No way!" said Florence. "I must get on that plane today. Let us keep moving down to the airport. This is just a tropical storm. It will be gone soon!"

"Sorry madam. This part of the road crosses the mountains, where the storms linger. They take longer to pass. What would you want me to do then, madam?"

In a low tone, the only words that Florence was able to utter were: "I don't know...".

What is Mindfulness?

The term "Mindfulness" has its roots in ancient Buddhist and Hindu teachings and practices. It is a rough translation from the ancient language Pali into English of the concept of sati. Sati encompasses attention, awareness, and being, and is considered a first step toward enlightenment[2].

In the past few years, mindfulness has become increasingly popular in Western cultures and has gained enormous projection and hype: a simple search using your favourite engine will produce hundreds of millions of references – an indication that the term is being used for meaning just about anything, serving as a multi-purpose "qualifier" of the most diverse practices and services.

Common meanings popularly and incorrectly associated with the term range from "meditation" to "well-being" to "Eastern Medicine," to name but a few of the more frequently heard. Given this state-of-affairs, caution is a must for anyone wishing to learn, to practice, or to apply the wise concepts and techniques from ancient Eastern cultures in the context of Western societies.

Let's take a closer look at the challenges involved, the first one being to have a proper definition of the term "mindfulness".

To help us to distinguish the critical attributes of "mindfulness", Susan David[3] suggests that we start by looking at its opposite: "mindlessness", which she defines as "state of unawareness and autopilot – you're not really present".

When we consider the key elements of David's definition of "mindlessness", it becomes clear that serious risks and consequences are to be expected. Unawareness – meaning the absence of knowledge or perception of the real aspects of any given situation or fact – can put at risk our capacity to notice, interpret, make sense of, decide, or act appropriately upon the issues at hand. Autopilot – meaning the automatic, un-reflected alignment to circumstances, commitments, objectives, and priorities that may have been relevant or useful in stable and predictable environments at one point in time – will significantly increase the risk of misalignment and unwanted results even in relatively stable situations.

"Mindlessness" is surely dangerous, but David's provocative approach sheds some light on what we should be looking for in a good definition of Mindfulness. We will get back to that later.

"Mindfulness" has already been the subject of serious studies and academic research. One of the pioneers of this research is Jon Kabat-Zinn[4].

Kabat-Zinn studied mindfulness under several Buddhist teachers, such as Philip Kapleau and Thich Nhat Hanh. As a professor at the University of Massachusetts Medical School in the late 1970s, he developed a program called Mindfulness-Based Stress Reduction (MBSR) to treat chronic pain – illustrating one of the first successful applications of Mindfulness to relevant issues and problems in a scientific domain. Following in the footsteps of Kabat-Zinn, a growing scientific community is focused on researching and developing applications of Mindfulness in the most diverse domains.

For example, Dan Goleman and neuroscientist Richard Davidson[5] sifted through hundreds of studies on mindfulness and similar practices and identified four benefits of mindfulness: stronger focus, staying calmer under stress, better memory, and good corporate citizenship.

Goleman and Davidson thus encourage us to think of mindfulness as a way of enhancing certain kinds of mental fitness, just as regular workouts at the gym build physical fitness.

Distilled from Goleman's work, many authors have published studies and conveyed practical experiences focusing on the application of mindfulness practices to the development of leadership and management competencies.

One good example is Maria Gonzalez: in her book[6] she defends that true leadership comes from within, from a place of deep calm and focus, that allows one to respond to any situation as it arises. To access that internal space, she then introduces some basic practices and techniques of mindfulness and then defines how to use them to develop the nine key attributes that, from her perspective, illustrate mindful leadership: Presence, Awareness, Calmness, Focus, Clarity, Equanimity, Positivity, Compassion and Impeccability.

Another good example is provided by Janice Marturano[7], an experienced leader and executive. Her approach is based on the concept of "bandwidth": "As leaders we need bandwidth ... the capacity to see, feel, hear, and reflect on what is in front of us and what is inside of us. When we have that space, we can deal with even an urgent problem in a calm, creative, and humane way, rather than have an expedient reaction to the pressure." She presents easy-to-use examples of mindfulness practices that can improve leadership performance and employee well-being.

We will now offer two examples of the implementation of company-wide programs integrating mindfulness and leadership practices in practical applications to the corporate and business world.

The Search Inside Yourself (SIY) program at Google

In 2007, one of Google's early engineers, Chade-Meng Tan, gathered a team of leading experts in mindfulness techniques, neuroscience, leadership, and emotional intelligence to develop an internal course for Google employees called *Search Inside Yourself (SIY)*. The aim of SIY was to help people develop the skills of mindfulness, empathy, compassion, and overall emotional intelligence to create conditions for individuals and groups to thrive.

Tan described this experience in his book[8] and his approach is now being implemented in other large corporations and is available to the general public.

The Ernst & Young (EY) Mindful Leadership Program

The Ernst & Young Mindful Leadership Program - a structured methodology for developing mindfulness in 8 weeks - is another example of the integration of Mindfulness concepts and practices within a corporate Leadership Development program.

Created by Clif Smith and described in *"Mindfulness without the bells and beads"[9]*, the program had as one of its key aspects the reframing of mindfulness as *"a set of techniques for wellness outside the scope of a learning organization"* into *"a way to impact performance, leadership and well-being in a unique way"*.

The examples above illustrate the effectiveness of mindfulness approaches in corporate and business settings and for business leaders and workers alike.
So what do we have to do to be mindful leaders?

The MYPRISM Model of Mindfulness

The works of Gonzalez, Marturano, Google, and EY mentioned above illustrate good approaches to apply the concepts of mindfulness to leadership and management challenges.

In MYPRISM, our approach to the application of mindfulness to leadership and management practices is structured through the practical integration of four pillars:

- **Awareness:** to identify and segment the aspects of our internal conditions as well as of our external environment that should be brought to consciousness.

- **Focus:** the deliberate, intentional orientation of our attention to the aspects relevant to our purpose, goal, or situation.

- **Practice:** the processes needed to prepare for purposeful decision making and action.

- **Reflection:** an intentional questioning and debrief of our experiences so that learnings can be incorporated into our repertoire as mindful leaders.

Let us then explore each of these four pillars.

Awareness & Focus: from Unconsciousness to Presence

> *"Consciousness gives us the opportunity for choice and change"*
>
> *(Daniel J. Siegel)*[10]

> *"Awareness is the state of being conscious of something. More specifically, it is the ability to directly know and perceive, to feel, or to be cognizant of events."*
>
> *(Wikipedia)*[11]

We have already discussed the risks of navigating in autopilot mode in today's increasingly unstable environments and complex leadership challenges. We also discussed the need to increase our perception or knowledge of the real facets of any given situation or fact.

So let us explore now what we can do to be more present for ourselves and the world around us. For that purpose, we will use the foundations developed and established by psychologist and leading expert in awareness and presence Daniel J. Siegel[12]:

> "The general term presence can be used ... for the notion of showing up in awareness and being receptive to what is happening...".

> "... when our minds wander unintentionally we are not present, we are not receptively aware, we are not mindful...".

> "... mental presence is a state of being wide awake and receptive to what is happening, as it is happening in the moment, within us and between the world and us..."

To increase our awareness and consciousness, we must identify what are the aspects - the "things" or "objects" in ourselves and in our environment – that we must be aware of to increase our capacity as leaders to notice, interpret, make sense of, decide, or act appropriately upon the issues at hand.

As described in his book[13], Siegel created a tool to address this need and named it the "Wheel of Awareness", which is "...a visual metaphor for the way the mind works... to help expand the container of consciousness... which is our subjective sense of knowing and includes both the knowing and the known..."[14].

Siegel also addresses the role of attention in the regulatory process of our mind, which leads us now to address the importance of focused attention in presence and mindful leadership.

A primary task of leadership is to direct attention, which, according to Dan Goleman[15], involves leaders learning to focus their own attention. To do so, Goleman suggests, leaders should group attention into three broad buckets: *focusing on yourself, focusing on others, and focusing on the wider world.*

As Goleman explains, by *focusing on oneself*, leaders develop their self-awareness (of sensations, feelings, emotions, etc.) and self-control (for example, cognitive control), which positively impacts their performance as leaders. *Focusing on others* means exercising a foundation of empathy and the ability to build social relationships – the second and third pillars of emotional intelligence. In sum, focusing inward and focusing constructively on others helps leaders cultivate the primary elements of emotional intelligence[16].

By *focusing on the longer term and on wider perspectives*, the inquisitive mind of leaders will explore new possibilities and advantages, inspiring them to disengage from the routine in order to roam widely and pursue fresh paths[17].

Integrating the concepts of focused attention and some of the concepts of the "Wheel of Awareness", we developed a *"Map of Objects of Awareness & Focus"* for our mindful leadership journey within MYPRISM.

In our *"Map of Objects"* model, there are four groups of objects. For each of these objects, we need to be acutely aware of their finer details and surroundings so that our journey will have a higher probability of success.

It is like navigating with a map. The more aware we are about the details on the map, our intended destination, and the signs and postings along the way, the more likely we will get to our destination. If we don't pay attention (if we are not mindful), we may get lost and be moving in the wrong direction.

Map of Objects of Awareness & Focus

In the MYPRISM map, there are four groups of objects:

1. Body Awareness & Focus

- Senses, sensations

2. Feelings & Emotions Awareness & Focus

- Feelings
- Emotions

3. Mental / Thinking Awareness & Focus

- Context
- Overall Mission
- Thoughts
- Point of View / Perspective
- Zoom In / Zoom Out
- Past / Present / Future
- Others' Perspectives

4. Relationship Awareness & Focus with

- other people,
- the environment,
- the situations and anything else outside

Now that we are aware of the objects on the *Map of Awareness & Focus*, what do we have to do to develop and achieve our awareness and focus? Practice is the answer.

Practice & Reflection: from Possibility to Mastery

We set out below exercises for each of these 4 groups of objects of Awareness & Focus for your "PRACTICE and REFLECTION".

In our recent work on Resilience[18] we developed tools and exercises that address the "objects of awareness" that we have just described, and have applied them in our executive coaching and mentoring work with senior leaders. We have broadened and extended those resources to integrate them into MYPRISM.

A - Practice & Reflection: Body Awareness & Focus

Exercise 1: Breathe to Reclaim Your Brain

In most situations of anxiety or threat, our lives are not at stake. It would thus be more helpful to all concerned if we were able to reclaim our brain and heart and face any threat with calm, clear, strategic thinking[19]. While pausing to get grounded, notice your breath. Intentionally breathe deeply and slowly (inhaling for four seconds and exhaling for six) at least three times. Physiologically, this is necessary to re-engage the prefrontal cortex; slow, regular breathing causes the vagus nerve to slow the heart rate during exhalation and helps control anxiety, anger, and other heightened survival emotions.

Questions

1. What is the pace of my breathing?

2. How deep are my breaths?

3. When I breathe deeply, where do I feel the tension?

4. What happens when I breathe directly into that seat of discomfort?

B - Practice & Reflection: Feelings & Emotions Awareness & Focus

Exercise 2: Get Grounded

Your emotional reaction is exactly that: YOURS. Getting grounded means sinking your feet squarely into the ground upon which you are standing now. Listen deeply to the voices in your head and the messages from your whole self.

Questions

1. What am I feeling? What is going on inside?
2. What am I focusing on?
3. If I act based upon those feelings, will that serve me (or other stakeholders)?
4. What do I want to happen versus what is happening?
5. What are the stakes? Who are the stakeholders?
6. Is this life or death?
7. How aligned are my reactions with my values?
8. How aligned are my reactions with the vision I/ we hold for myself? My team? My organization? The stakeholders?
9. What other emotions are available to me now?
10. What problem am I trying to solve?
11. What if there is no concrete solution?
12. What do I believe to be true about the challenge?
13. What if those beliefs/ assumptions are wrong?

Exercise 3: Self-awareness – The Five C's

Honing your mindfulness muscle will always start with a focus on self-awareness. This will allow you to focus on five

Cs: calm, clear, curious, courageous, and compassionate. We are convinced that developing and using these five perspectives will help leaders to develop their own mindfulness capability – and to make skilful decisions as opposed to resorting to reactive impulses. As a result, they will rebound more quickly from shock or impact, and the odds of growing from the experience will increase.

Questions:

Calm:

- On a scale to 1 to 10 (with ten being the most calm) how calm am I now?
- What is helping me from not slipping 1 number down? What would make me move 1 number up?

Clear:

- What is happening now? Not yesterday, not potentially in the future, but at this very moment?
- What do I need to know now? If I don't have that knowledge, what do I need to believe?
- Is it clear to others who and what I need to be now?

Curious:

- What is the one additional question I could ask, even if I think I know the answer already?
- Who might disagree with me?
- What might be possible?

Compassionate:

- Am I being compassionate/kind to myself?
- How might others be coping with this?
- How might I help given what I have/where I am?

Courageous:

- Where am I on my 4 Cs above?

- What do I fear will happen if I were to take action?

- What do I fear will happen if I were not to take action?

What action should/can I take or not take despite my fear?

C – Practice & Reflection: Mental/Thinking Awareness & Focus

Exercise 4: What is Really Going on Here?

We live in the past, present, and future simultaneously. We take our past with us. Our present is where we are now. We are in yesterday's future. How does it all fit together? What is the momentum underlying this moment? How can we be present in, and objective about, this moment, in order to impact what the future (tomorrow, next week, month, year) could look like?

Questions:

1. What if I could only make the right decision?

2. What is the big picture?

3. What is the momentum underlying this moment?

4. How does this all fit together?

5. What is the next step that I can take with confidence and clarity at this moment?

6. What if I am exactly where I am supposed to be regardless of the outcome?

7. What do I not want to see? What are my blind spots?

8. How can I view this as an opportunity instead of a problem?

9. Who do you want to be right now for yourself and for others who depend upon your leadership?

Exercise 5: Ride the Wave to Shore

Like water, time and momentum alone will carry you through, under, over, or around the disturbance. The question is, what will your state of mind be during that period? Will you be buffeted around by the force of the situation? Or will you have the presence of mind to navigate, innovate, and discover what could be helpful along the way?

Questions:

1. What do I have control over?

2. What is outside of my control?

3. What am I seeing or encountering that I have never seen before?

4. What else do I need to know before I make a decision?

5. What are others thinking? Whose opinion do I value?

6. What are my assumptions and how can I test those?

7. What do I need in order to let go of the things I cannot control?

8. What are my, and only my, responsibilities here?

9. What am I resisting that is getting in the way of flowing with the situation?

10. Who do I need to be for my team? My organization? For others who turn to me as a "life raft"?

Exercise 6: Capture and Use the Heat of the Moment

A mindful leader develops the ability to take advantage of the heat of the moment, the emotional power of the discomfort underlying our drive to survive and thrive.

Questions:
1. Why do I find myself in this situation?
2. What lessons could this situation hold?
3. How could this experience become a benefit for me if I manage it well?
4. What consequences will be avoided if I can lead myself (and my team) through this well?
5. What would be the impact of managing this challenge well?
6. What is my best, most competent self being called to do?
7. What in this experience drives and motivates me to survive and thrive?

Exercise 7: Looking Inward

Looking inward will help you understand why you are on your learning journey, and how you're showing compassion, forgiveness, and accountability, key qualities of a mindful leader.

Questions:
1. What does it mean to be an effective leader?
2. What does self-leadership mean?
3. What does "success" look like?
4. Where am I on my learning journey?
5. What does mindfulness mean to me?
6. What does a mindful leader look like?
7. When I am being mindful, what is going on inside?
8. When I am being mindful, what does that look like? What do I do?
9. What trigger(ed) me to turn on my mindfulness?

10. What were my concerns?

11. What did I most fear could happen?

12. Are the ways I show up as mindful consistent with my "best self"?

13. Is the mindful leader I am now the same person as the mindful leader I aspire to be?

14. Who do I want to be?

15. Who is this situation calling me to be?

16. When have I experienced a situation like this before?

17. What worked well?

18. What did not work?

19. How is this situation similar/different from other situations?

20. What insights would be helpful to re-apply?

21. What would be harmful?

22. What are the opportunities here to grow? Improve?

23. On a scale of 1 to 10, how ashamed am I feeling that I am in a situation that I do not know how to handle?

24. On a scale of 1 to 10, how compassionate am I feeling toward myself? 25. What would I say to a friend if they were in a similar situation?

D - Practice & Reflection: Relationship Awareness & Focus

Exercise 10: Looking Outward

Looking outward very much focuses you on your impact and helps you to identify new practices as they might be needed, or a new narrative to guide you into the next steps.

Questions:

1. What impact or outcome am I intending to achieve with others?

2. Does my mindfulness behaviour create a positive impact on others?

3. In these high-alert situations:

   a. Am I fostering engagement?

   b. Am I making space for collaboration?

   c. Am I supporting teamwork?

   d. Am I allowing for others' courage, creativity, and innovation?

4. Who can I trust to give me honest feedback?

5. What are my values and how can I align them with the decisions I have to make?

Conclusion

We shall not cease from exploration
And the end of all our exploring
Will be to arrive where we started
And know the place for the first time.
T. S. Eliot [20]

As we all know, becoming a mindful leader is a lifelong journey, which means that we will always have to be intentionally curious and attentive to ourselves and to the world around us.

In this chapter, we have described this journey into mindful leadership along two fundamental and interconnected paths: one from Unconsciousness to Presence, the other from Possibility to Mastery.

The journey from Unconsciousness to Presence is propelled by two key engines - Awareness and Focus - which intentionally target the objects and provide the guiding lights relevant to every step along the way.

In the journey from Possibility to Mastery, we use Practice and Reflection as the generators that continuously produce the more-and-more elaborate energies required to move and progress along the journey.

We believe that if we use MYPRISM as a regular practice and as an additional GPS (Global Positioning System) in our individual journeys, we will enable the means by which we can have more positive impact, both on ourselves and on our relational and physical environments.

A key and inspirational mindset that has been nurtured by the authors along the way is that of the "Reflective Practitioner". Created by MIT professor Donald Schön[21], the "reflection-in-action" practice has inspired us along our professional careers to produce frameworks, methods and tools that can be seen as anchored in Prof. Schön's "epistemology of practice" philosophical perspective.

The beauty of mindful leadership is that we have as many opportunities to develop it as we have seconds in our lives: every moment brings in itself the possibility of learning and growth and it is up to each one of us to do something to benefit from it.

We believe that a framework like MYPRISM will help you as a leader to exercise Leadership in a more Mindful way.

Key Take-Aways from this Chapter

Considering the development journey as a mindful leader, we will now provide some additional reflections about mindfulness with a technique that uses a "storytelling" perspective: What, So What, Now What.

This technique will help you to differentiate "facts" from "judgements" from "actions", therefore providing an organizing frame that favours learning.

You can use the questions in various ways: periodically, before or after some specific event or milestone, after some impactful situation, or whenever you feel like reflecting.

The questions that follow will serve as a starting point for your further reflections about your own mindful leadership journey.

The "What" Questions:

The "What" questions will help you to screen, identify, and name or describe facts, feelings, sensations, emotions, thoughts, perspectives, relationships, and other items of the **"Map of Objects of Awareness and Focus"** presented above.

You may expand this list of questions so that you shape and adjust your reflection and learning process to your own style and preferences. Make it your list of questions.

The "So What" Questions:

The "So What" questions will help you analyze and think critically about the responses to the "What" questions and will help you in the process of "sense-making" about the "what happened" by identifying the impacts that the answers to the "What" questions had on you.

The "Now What" Questions:

The "Now What" questions will help you express the attitudes or actions that are applicable after the reflections triggered by the "What" and "So What", questions and can also be used to summarize actions going forward.

The "What", "So What" and "Now What" questions can be organized in tables for reference and further reflection.

To summarize the key learnings of the reflection exercises proposed above, we can use the following questions:

- What are the two or three things that I did this time that I will do again?

- What are the two or threethings that I did not do this time that I will do next time?

- What are the two or three things that I did this time that I should not do next time?

CHAPTER 3

"Y" is for Why

Amnezza (not his real name) is one of the highest-producing partners of a global investment bank. He rose from the most junior analyst to the head of the firm's M&A practice and became the youngest partner in the firm's history. In a culture of "up or out", every partner is up for review every three years. This was his year for review. He needed to produce numbers, show a strong pipeline, and ace the 360 performance review that included contributions to mentoring. Meeting his numbers was not a problem. In fact, he would once again "exceed expectations". Amnezza had a strong track record of rainmaking for the firm. So what if he did not get straight A's in his 360 review? So what if he was perceived as a bully by his peers, scary by his team, and cold by his managers. He was once again "going up, not out". Yet, somehow all that did not feel right. *Why am I so easily wound up all the time? It is stressful and very tiring.*, he thought to himself. He had all the symbols of success, including a loving spouse, three happy children, a swank modern apartment in the city, and a sprawling second home in the country, and he was still outpacing people years younger in his running club. Yet the questions kept coming. *"Why are people in the office so put off by me? Don't they know that's how I make them successful?" "Why am I the way I am in the office vs. the way I am at home?" "Why am I even asking why?"*

The answers to Amnezza's questions turn on helping him understand the "why" behind his behaviour on two levels. On one level, he needs to develop a deep awareness of the drivers of his behaviour: Why does he react the way he does? What is affecting his behaviour choices? At a deeper level, he needs to be clear about his wider purpose and what he wants to be and how he is living his values on a daily basis. In this chapter, we will discuss the cognitive process behind the "why" of our behavioural choices. By throwing more light on the "why question" (or "Y" in MYPRISM), we hope that asking "why" can be a source of empowerment rather than a roadblock.

The way we are wired: "WHY" is the brain seeking answers

Our discussion of "WHY" (or "Y") starts with understanding how the human brain is wired to constantly seek answers to make sense of the situations confronting us. If we have answers, we feel more assured of our survival. Without answers, we feel threatened.

We know from our own behaviour that our brain seeks safety, comfort, and pleasure by default. Very few of us proactively seek out danger (and even those who do see "danger" as fun). Even fewer of us would choose long term uncertainty over certainty. Indeed, scientific studies identified a part of our brain[1] called the amygdala that appears to drive the motivation to seek pleasure, harmony, and avoid pain.

When we perceive a threat or danger, the amygdala part of the human brain releases stress hormones to prepare us to fight or flee or freeze. This is our instinct to survive, to not be destroyed. This part of our brain also regulates memory, emotional response (such as fear and anxiety), as well as decision making. The brain has learned that pain is mostly avoided if we repeat a behaviour from the past that did not lead to pain. The brain becomes more and more efficient in recognizing this pattern. Over time, it looks for and craves certainty because certainty is a sign of safety, which, in turn, brings comfort. We fear what we don't know is both a cliché and a scientific statement. Studies have shown, for example, that children raised in monocultures develop low intercultural awareness and tolerance in adulthood. Simultaneously, our brain avoids any signs or symbols that it associates with discomfort or danger, such as putting a hand on a hot stove. We learn very early on in childhood that is not a thing to do.

In short, our brain is essentially wired to work on a spectrum of *survival instincts*: from one end which seeks *pleasure* in the form of familiarity and security', to the other end which avoids threats and pain. The complexity lies in the fact we can be in pleasure and in pain in the same experience. The challenge is how to regulate our behaviour (or action) towards the identified reward purposefully rather than default to an emotional reaction.

Level 1 "WHY": Serving the purpose of the moment

Given our predisposition towards comfort and pleasure, it is not surprising that when our actions or other people's actions do not result in the outcome we desire, our first instinct is to try to bend the environment to our will.

We may not immediately realize, however, that when we are stressed, our cognitive capabilities become impaired. Our amygdala kicks into high gear. In this mental state, we default to our instincts more than to our cognitive skills. We make decisions based on impulse – an emotional reaction, rather than a purposeful response. How many times have we come to regret impulsive reactions to a situation?

Let's pick a scenario that we have all experienced at some point of our lives: "This service agent is being rude to me" or "I don't deserve to be treated like this". These thoughts arise because rudeness is not what you expect and when that happens your brain signals to you to reject it. The "fight" mode of your brain is engaged because it has learned that rudeness is a "threat". If you are not mindful of what your brain is doing, it will guide you to default to an impulsive reaction to defend or protect your being. You choose to "fight". We can all imagine how the "fight" mode will react to that rudeness.

Instead of "fighting", take a moment to remind yourself of your intentions and objectives, and to allow yourself to accept the reality of the situation. You may discover that rudeness has nothing to do with you. You are not giving in to the rudeness (or any adversity you are facing). Rather, you are accepting what has already happened, and anchoring your behaviour to your intentions and purpose. You are switching your fight mode to the creative mode to find a pathway to achieve your original purpose. Directly fighting a reality over which you have no control is futile and indeed a maladaptive behaviour. The rudeness will not be removed by your anger. Your anger in fact fuels that rudeness – the exact opposite of your desired outcome.

Returning to our example of the rude service agent, your purpose might be to catch the next available flight out of the crowded airport. The agent was just rude to you. You can choose to respond with your own rudeness, which will likely cause the agent to be less willing to be helpful or creative. Or you can choose instead to show some kindness and patience (e.g., with sympathizing remarks such as "this must be hell for you today dealing with this crowd"), which is more likely to yield a positive result. We may never know what was going on with the rude agent, but at that tense moment, your objective is to get on that plane, not pass judgment on the agent. Why focus your energy on that rudeness? Why not navigate towards your objective based on what you can control instead? Which course of action will bring you closer to your purpose vs. depleting you further?

Serving to save a match point: the purpose of the moment

Ever wonder how world class tennis champions keep their nerves when they are one point from defeat and need to save a match point with their serve? They can do this because they are able to hone their cognitive skills to harness their emotions, and then choose an action that is purposeful rather than surrendering to the stress of the moment. They do not reject their anxiety. Rather, they accept it but have the ability not to be hijacked by it. This is an example of the mindfulness that we alluded to in the previous chapter. Mindfulness starts by being aware of (and kind to) your own anxieties. When you are kind to your anxieties, your stress automatically calms down. This takes practice. It is the practice of being mindful of your environmental and internal conditions. That is how top athletes continue to perform at their peak despite the stress of the moment. They do not reject the stress. Instead, they acknowledge it and return to the sources of their strength and calm by remembering their skills from years of training.

The next time you are anxious, instead of asking, "Why is this happening?", try mindfully reminding yourself of your intentions and purpose by asking: "What is my desired outcome from this situation?" and "What would give me calm and wisdom to address what is happening". When you mindfully return to your intentions and purpose, you will find that your anxiety almost immediately goes down. Mindfulness reduces the stress of a situation, and when we feel less stressed, our cognitive skill improves. We start to see other ways to find comfort and strength. In the case of our tennis champion, this is the moment when their cognitive abilities kick in despite the stress, and they see what new strategies should be adopted to save that match point. Remember, champions don't let the environment derail them from their objectives. Re-centre your internal conditions to respond to your external conditions, always anchoring your behavioural choices to your original intention and purpose.

Let's go back to Amnezza. During his coaching sessions, he reflected on moments when his temper was triggered at work – such as the time a colleague failed to deliver on an assignment, which put an important deal at risk.

> *Triggering event: external environment not what he expected.*
>
> *Default reaction: Remove the threat. Reject the failure. Scold. Blame.*
>
> *Likely result: Fear, anxiety, risk of mistake not diminished. Resentment from his team.*

During coaching, he was invited to reflect on his desired outcome: an urgent solution. What could be an alternative behavioural choice that was more likely to achieve this outcome?

> *Triggering event: external environment not what he expected*
>
> *Over-ridden response: Pause. What is my intended outcome? What can be done to reverse the error? If not, what else can be done to remediate and advance the goal?*

> *Actual result: Creative problem solving. Speed of resolution. Risk reduced that mistake is repeated. Earned the respect of his team.*

Amnezza's purpose of the moment was to close the deal. Yelling at his team did not align with what would have gotten them closer to the purpose, nor was it consistent with his values. His default reaction was to yell because the situation deviated from his desired outcome. That was the level one "why". Once he understood that and acknowledged that trigger, he was more able to regulate his behaviour choice. He learned that when he stopped yelling, his team performed better. The latter behavioural choice brought him closer to his intended outcome (his purpose of the moment).

Level 2 "WHY": Purpose and Values

Humans are amongst the few living creatures on earth that seek to influence the environment based on their needs. Here, we are referring to both physiological and emotional needs. Physiological needs are easier to identify. When we feel warm, we turn on the AC. When we are thirsty, we drink. And so forth. If we are clear about what moves us, we will be more able to tailor our actions to align with these needs. However, what we think we need may not always be intuitively obvious. Emotional needs are particularly tricky. What is the authentic source of our motivation? This is the deeper level of "why". In the early stage of his coaching, Amnezza articulated "why" as *I work to provide a good life to the people I love*. That seems clear enough. However, over time, even with this clear purpose, Amnezza found his level of motivation waning. His enthusiasm for work was definitely not the same as when he first started his career. *"I work to provide a good life to the people I love"* motivated him early in his career, but once that need was met, the power of this "why" as a source of motivation weakened. What else might be happening? This "why" was no longer fuelling an unmet need.

There are at least two powerful studies that can help us understand our psychological needs. First, the Gestalt School of Thought[2] suggests that humans seek closure, familiarity, and logic.

What we do must make "sense" to our being. If not, we struggle with finding the motivation to continue. Edward Deci and Richard Ryan's Theory of Self-Determination[3] identified three psychological needs that, if unmet, diminish our mental well-being and therefore our cognitive abilities. These three needs are autonomy, competence, and connectedness. Perhaps, for example, Amnezza did not feel *connected* to his job even though he was successful at it?

Remember, seeking answers to the "why" question is the foundation of what drives us as humans. Amnezza may not have been aware that his brain was looking for an answer for his lack of connectedness to the work he was doing. Our "why" relates to our values, the ultimate source of our behavioural choices. Through a series of psychometric assessments, Amnezza discovered that one of his values was helping others grow. His psychometric assessments helped him see, also, that he actually enjoyed being recognized as wise. During his coaching sessions, he was invited to reflect on the actions that might be aligned with those values. How could he live his values at work? As a successful leader at the bank, following his values led him to mentoring the next generation of bankers for

...ause he saw so much of himself in them. With ...tion, he was able to find renewed energy by ...g which aspects of his job were most aligned with ...es and which would meet his instinctive human ...or connectedness. He started living his values and ...behaviours in turn changed how others perceived ... His work relationships developed into deeper trusting ...endships and mentorship. Asking "why" helped Amnezza ...ediscover his motivation and modify his behavioural choices.

"Y" as your source of motivation

Have you ever wondered why you seem to be motivated to perform certain activities but not others. How, despite your initial enthusiasm for a new year resolution, you deviate from it and finally abandon it altogether? How certain behaviour choices seem more difficult than others? Losing weight always seems more difficult than, say, getting involved in local charities. The research of Deci and Ryan is again insightful in determining why our level of motivation may vary.

Deci and Ryan's work made the distinction between intrinsic and extrinsic motivation. Intrinsic motivation happens when the activity itself is a source of validation and joy. The activity itself is the reward. The best example of intrinsic motivation in action is watching children play. The sheer energy to continue the activity is intrinsic. We certainly don't have to encourage children to play. Athletes or artists experience significant intrinsic motivation. Even if there were no medals or monetary returns, many will still play a sport or learn a musical instrument.

The other type of motivation, according to Deci and Ry-

an's research, is extrinsic motivation. This happens whe
we are performing an activity in pursuit of a reward. Work
ing for a wage is a frequent example. Other forms of extrinsic motivation may be when we perform an activity because
we believe that it is expected of us[4] (e.g., going to church
or making the bed). This is true even if the activity aligns
with our values but does not truly energize us[5]. "I will do
it, but I am not really getting joy from it" is how, for example, we might think about volunteering to raise funds for
a charity. It is important to realize that extrinsic motivations are inherently unstable and not sustainable, chiefly
because these extrinsic motivations undermine our sense
of "autonomy". Studies show that unless we genuinely do
something out of our own volition (or at least we believe
we chose to do it), our motivation will diminish as soon
as the conditions pushing us to perform deteriorate. For
example, after a certain level (or at a certain stage in adult
development), salary becomes less of a motivator than other, more intrinsic values. That is why "WHY" is important
to base our behavioural choices on our values. It is the
surest way to sustain our authenticity and performance
level. Working for a high wage was definitely aligned with
Amnezza's purpose to provide a good life for his family. The
money, however, only motivated him up to an extent. Over
time, it started to undermine his autonomy. He started
to feel that working for money was perhaps not what he
wanted to do but what he had to do. To reverse the depletion of his motivation, he needed to realize that his job
provided him more than money; it was also in many ways
aligned to his other values.

With mindful practice over time, we can increasingly
anchor our behavioural choices in our values and intentions. You may be surprised that the next time an airline

rude to you, instead of being triggered and ...cked", you are more able to remain calm and ...cause you are mindful that it is not your inten- ...iticize or be angry but to get on that plane!

...rriding the anxious "Y" with the ...ious "Y"

...ne wonderous thing about the way we are wired is that we can hone our cognitive skills to override our default anxious "Y" and arrive at a purposeful, positive behavioural response. When we are mindfully aware of our emotional condition and acknowledge the threat (just like our tennis champion serving to save a match point), we will be able to unleash another powerful side of our brain: the learning side. This is the curious side of that "Y" question. Relying on our curious brain is a more uplifting way to navigate our way out of distress.

As we discussed above, asking questions is an inevitable human brain function. This intellect sets us apart in the animal kingdom. In addition to seeking information for survival, we also ask questions out of sheer curiosity. Humans (more than most living creatures) have a genuine yearning to explore, discover, *and* elevate our existence. This to a large extent explains the allure and importance of art in human civilization. Scientists call this "epistemic curiosity"[6] and it is intrinsic to our human nature. Epistemic curiosity can help us avoid rumination and drive us towards the creativity to explore options and find solutions. While our anxious brain leads us to maladaptive behaviour, curiosity leads to excitement and openness. We are filled with positive energy because we perceive and indeed receive a reward from this curiosity.

Notice how quickly a jilted broken heart recovers once it becomes intrigued by another love interest? The break-up still happened but now the energy around it is suddenly very different. This is the magic and power of the curious brain.

Looking within for answers vs. looking outside

How familiar are the following statements: "The world is a great place if I achieve *my* objectives, *my* goals." "Everything is going *my* way." "Life sucks when I don't get what I want." We spend a lot of energy trying to change the world and get around obstacles to satisfy our needs or desires (recall the brain's innate need to make sense of our environment in order to feel safe.) Perhaps, if we acknowledge that our world is in fact a reflection of us, and if we focus our energy on our *own* actions rather than the actions of others, we might be more able to influence the environment around us. Back to the case of the rude service agent: We can choose to ask, "Why is/are he/she/they so rude?" vs. "What can I do to remove/reduce that rudeness?". The first approach is our attempt to force the world into our emotional reality. The second is a more skilful way to influence the world through our own mindful behaviour. When we project positive energy, the world around us will reflect that energy back at us. The world is indeed a mirror of what we project.[7]

This following story is a Taoist teaching originated by the ancient Chinese philosopher Zhuang Zhou. A boatman was rowing to cross a fast-flowing river. Suddenly, he saw another boat heading his way. He started shouting at the other boat to change course. Our boatman became more agitated when his shouting was ignored. He started to curse at the other boat. Before he knew it, the oncoming boat collided with him and with the force of the river, he tipped over. As he was falling into the river, he noticed that the other boat was empty. There was no one to be angry with or to blame for his falling. His fury was replaced by a sense of sheepishness as he climbed his way back into his own boat and continued to row across to the opposite bank quietly. The empty boat continued to float away. Deepak Chopra famously asked his class once, "There are many empty boats out there. How many are you going to yell at?"

Just the thought of there being someone to blame for his imminent accident made this ancient boatman angry. The moment he realized that there was no one to blame, his anger evaporated. This parable has been used to convey many teachings. The most powerful is that we should first look towards ourselves and focus on observing what *we* are contributing to the situation before we expend energy on blaming others. In the case of the boatman, perhaps if he had focused on what he could do to avoid the collision, he would have saved himself much angst and gotten home drier and faster. Before you shout at another empty vessel, ask yourself a silent question: "What can I change about myself in order to achieve my goals, given the situation that I am in?" As you moderate your actions, you will find that your world changes with you. This next time things don't work out the way you had planned, reflect on what you need to change about yourself first before you charge around trying to change the workplace in a hurried fury.

A word of caution on asking "why"

Asking "why" without curiosity can be depleting. The best example of a "depleting why" is rumination. We have all done that – we go through over and over again in our minds what cudda/wudda/shudda happened. "Why didn't I get that promotion?" "What did I do wrong?" "If I had said this or done that?". Merely asking questions without invoking learning and change is not helpful. Indeed, it can lead to a dangerous downward spiral. Taken to the extreme and if not corrected, we may subconsciously repeat a hurtful experience over and over again in our mind as a form of survival. Our brain is trying to soothe us by finding an explanation for the hurt. If not redirected, the brain may mistakenly tell us that since we survived the trauma through pain and endurance, the way to continue to survive is to repeat the trauma. Freud called this "repetition compulsion".[8] So, how do we stop rumination?

Start with a positive "what" vs. a negative "why"

Our brain will always ask questions. There is no way to stop it from asking. Questions are the expression and tools of curiosity. And the brain always provides an answer – whether factual or fictional, the brain will provide one. We seek answers in order to establish structure, to find order in chaos. We find comfort in predictability because the unknown is potentially a threat to our survival. This explains why people fear what they don't know. We repeat actions that we believe will lead to a desired reward[9]. Based on our past experiences (and memories), we default to responses that helped us survive (or endure) in the past.

This impacts the way we look at things, which informs our behaviour. Our behaviour in turn reinforces our historical responses. So, unless we mindfully interrupt this cycle, we default to what we know. We default to what we learned from our past experience (our "autopilot") which may not be applicable to the present.

Behavioural scientists[10] have observed that our emotional states tend to be self-regulating. Our psychological and physiological states are either positive or negative. In a positive state, our blood pressure is lower, while our level of oxytocin (a.k.a. the love hormone) and our cognitive skills are enhanced (e.g., memory, learning). In a negative state, our emotions are largely guilt, shame, fear, and anxiety, and our cognitive skills are compromised (e.g., ability to focus only narrowly). If we start in a negative emotional state, it is likely that we will remain there until something else happens to disrupt it[11], and vice versa. This positive/negative state of mind[12] is the basis for a field of study broadly called "positive psychology". Positive psychology argues that starting from a position of strength is more likely to yield improvement and sustained psychological and physiological well-being.

What does all this mean? Because an emotional state is self-regulating and self-perpetuating, it is important to start with a positive state. If we are in a negative state, we should disrupt it with a positive stimulus. For example, instead of asking "How far have I fallen from my objectives?", ask yourself, "What have I done right to get me to where I am so far". As a leader, you can start a meeting with, "What do we like about this quarter's performance?" vs. "How are we doing in terms of financial targets this quarter?". You will notice that the energy of the room will be very different depending on which emotional stimulus you invoke.

Empower your "Y" instinct with "what"

We can reframe our instinctive, unstoppable "Y" to a "what" question to unleash our positive emotional state. Let's look at a few common examples:

Why am I not losing weight? What can I do to lose weight?

Why are they so disagreeable? What can I say to convince them?

Why is this happening? We had planned everything so well. What can I do now that things did not work out as planned?

Add your own in the next few lines as practice

As you practice reframing your "Why", you are honing your learning mind, which is always more creative and skilful than your anxious mind. You will see that the adversity you are facing is less insurmountable than you had imagined.

Using "Y" as a manner of self care and compassion

Let's take your "Y" practice to a higher level. We discussed earlier in this chapter that asking "why" is our brain's attempt to make sense of the situation. We talked about how our anxious brain is our default mode of response. Some behavioural scientists describe this as the "protector" part of our psychology taking hold while suppressing other emotions and cognitive functions[13]. It seems the sadder, angrier, and more hurt we feel, the more this protector part of our brain asserts itself by trying to control or change the environment. Perhaps that is why some angry people double down on their fury and become violent. Have you noticed how people who are stricken by extreme grief are very prone to blame their environment for their plight? In this state of mind, we take actions that are actually not healing our hurt or addressing our anger. Instead, we act out – for example, by losing our temper – to distract us from those emotions or to deny them.

Why is this protector brain so powerful? In most cultures, children are raised on value systems that treat emotions, such as crying and fear, as weaknesses. Impatience or anger from a child is met with punishment. It is therefore not surprising that we consider such feelings as "negative", and when they surface, our protector brain steps forward to quash them. Paradoxically, our survival instinct is to suppress the hurt rather than allow it to heal. We engage in other activities to eradicate or bury these emotions rather than pay attention to them. To heal these anxieties, we can begin with self-compassion. In the mindful practice that we discussed in Chapter 1, we talked about being mindfully aware of our internal conditions. One of the things we can do to start the healing process is to ask ourselves a few of the following questions to uncover the 'why' underlying your experience:

"What am I fearing?"

"What is it that I am angry or disappointed about?"

"What is the bad thing I think will happen next?"

If you really take time to think about these questions, you may be surprised by the answers that emerge. Let's take a look at another real case study[14] to illustrate this practice:

> Mary (again a pseudonym) is the CEO of
> a 20-year-old, $300M company. Being a

15-year-old veteran of the company, she cares passionately about the company's mission, employees, and customers. Indeed, many of the companies' values are synonymous with her personal ones. During the 2020 COVID lockdown, the entire company switched to remote working. After six months, her senior leadership team started to report signs of organization fatigue and employee burnout. Mary sprang into action, launching various initiatives to boost employee morale. Understanding the importance of building and maintaining team connectedness in a virtual environment, she launched "bring your own virtual lunch hour". She also launched personal birthday greetings each week to every employee. She flooded the company's intranet with uplifting stories. Her goal: to project a caring organization.

After a few weeks, it seemed none of these initiatives were working. Her managers continued to report a decrease in productivity. Worse, a few critical line managers quit, citing personal reasons. During one of her coaching sessions, she was asked: "What do you think would happen to you if your employees continue to be unresponsive to your initiatives". She replied without any hesitation: "Productivity will slide". The coach repeated the question, "What do you think would happen to you?". Mary paused and this time it took her some time before responding, "I guess I would feel that I failed". The coach persisted, "What do you think will happen to you if you fail?". She looked perplexed and replied tentatively, "I will not be respected and perhaps my status as their leader will be diminished."

After a few sessions, Mary came to realize that her drive to spring into quick action was driven by her own anxieties around failure. She needed to project resilience and decisiveness as the leader. Her intention was always to project kindness. After she acknowledged that no one on her team was judging her for failure, she changed her approach. She took time to be compassionate to herself first and when she had returned to a stronger, more creative frame of mind, she was able to recognize the different sources of stress that her employees were undergoing. Some had health worries, others had parental pressures, others had career uncertainties. Instead of initiating activities to lift their spirits, she started to ask them how they felt. Instead of "doing", she did more "asking" and "being with". She also started to share her own anxieties with her team. She became more compassionate to her anxieties and with it more compassionate towards her team. It turned out the "fix" Mary needed was easier than she thought. By being willing to be vulnerable to her team, she soothed her own anxieties and, in the process, deepened the respect and trust her team had for her. This in turn lifted them. The team bounced back stronger.

Let your values (rather than your emotions) guide your destiny

Mahatma Gandhi once said, "Watch your thoughts as they become your actions. Watch your actions for they become your habits. Watch your habits for they become your values and your values become your destiny". In other words, if you are not the master of your thoughts, you become a slave to your internal demons and you are no longer the master of your own destiny.

So, let's reverse the paradigm. Start with your values. Let them guide your actions which will become your habit. Over time, your behaviour reflects the way you think. You regain mastery over your destiny.

Let's bring back Amnezza, the person who started this chapter. He evolved from an anxious, angry, arrogant banker to a nurturing mentor and respected peer. He is still rich for sure, but he is a happier rich banker who is not depleted. Better yet, he is living his values on a daily basis and is respected at work and loved at home.

Key take-aways from this chapter

1. Asking "WHY" is human.

2. There are two sides of "WHY":

   a. The default form of the "WHY" question is the survival mode. If you don't disrupt this default mode, you risk going into a loop of maladaptive behaviour as you lose sight of the reality of your external environment. Paradoxically, this survival mode weakens your ability to navigate and emerge from adversity.

    b. Disrupting the default mode with mindfulness will unleash your innate curiosity and creativity to arrive at a more skilful response.

3. Reframing your "WHY" as a "WHAT" is an effective way to disrupt the default anxious mode. "What" is my intention or objective *at the moment*? This is your "Level 1 WHY".

4. "Y" is also the source of your motivation. It is the source of your energy and renewal. Intrinsic motivation is more sustainable than extrinsic motivation.

5. Your values are intrinsic to you. This is your "Level 2 WHY". Anchoring your behavioural choices in your values is a more productive expenditure of your emotional and physiological energy.

6. When your behaviours are guided by your values, you are more able to influence your environment rather than being enslaved by it.

7. Your intrinsic "Y" becomes your destiny. You will live your values and purpose fully.

CHAPTER 4

"P" is for
Perspective

One of our clients was part of a group of leaders. They directly reported to the CXO in a global firm and were seriously annoyed by how their boss led the function globally. The situation had escalated to the point that this group of leaders was ready to launch the corporate equivalent of a mutiny. A coach brought in to help diffuse the situation met with the group in a conference room on the top floor of a beautiful hotel near Lisbon/Portugal. The coach started the meeting by giving everyone time and space to vent; the flip chart papers filled very quickly. After four flipcharts, the coach felt that he had heard enough and said: "It seems that you have now listed what you thought was 'wrong' with Mike (not his real name). Now let's try to look at what you appreciate about Mike". Silence. The group heard the waves of the Atlantic Ocean gently roll onto the shore ten floors below. The coach sat quietly and waited. The beautiful sound of the waves was uninterrupted. Then one group member volunteered, "There was this situation the other day when I discussed something with Mike, and he came up with a very good idea ...". Someone else joined in. After 20 minutes, the group had filled three flipchart papers. Had the coach at that point asked the group to "write a letter to Mike mentioning all those things that you appreciate about him", that would have been a very nice letter, indeed!

That was a masterpiece of helping a group take on a different perspective.

In 1986, the British newspaper *The Guardian* used a video ad to make the same point; it was barely 30 seconds long and only needed three lines of copy:

An event seen from one point of view gives one impression.

Seen from another point of view, it gives quite a different impression.

But it is only when you get the whole picture that you can fully understand what is going on.

In the first take by a first camera (one point of view), you see a young man, whose style of dressing identifies him as a skinhead, running away from a car that is slowly moving. The two people inside the car are staring at the young man.

In the second take by a second camera (another point of view), you see the same young man running at full speed directly toward a man in a suit and tie with a briefcase.

And in the third take by a third camera (the whole picture), you see how the young man pushes the guy in a suit and tie away from the sidewalk and into an open door of a house before a load of stones falls from a crane ... landing exactly where the unsuspecting suited guy was standing just a second earlier.

In 30 seconds, this ad manages to drive home the key point that we are trying to make when talking about perspective. The perspective of the first camera presents a suspicious-looking person running away, and we wonder, has he done something wrong, has he committed a crime? The second camera presents someone who is in the process of attacking someone else, presumably a worthwhile target because he's so well dressed. The third camera, however, shows that the young man, contrary to beliefs created by the first two perspectives, has one intention only, and that is to save someone else from a very bad accident. Our beliefs and conclusions completely depend upon the perspective that we take, where we stand, physically and internally (with our state of mind), how we see an event, how we make sense of it, which meaning we attach to it, how we react to it, and what we will do next. Let us unpack these multiple options.

Why is perspective important?

We can live most of our lives by relying on the biological starting point for all our behaviours, which sits in what is often called the "reptilian brain". It is the home of our natural, instinctive reactions[1] to anything that happens to us and around us. In a social situation, for example, we might feel shame or guilt or the need to protect ourselves from something that is happening. In a webinar at the Institute of Coaching (IOC), Lisa Feldman Barrett[2] spoke about how emotions are made. We are designed biologically to make and check predictions as part of our sense-making of the input provided by our eyes, ears, and other senses. We try to find out what things mean, so that we can provide a response. Note that we say "provide", not "choose", a key difference: Most responses are "automatic", i.e., not based on an intention that we have consciously defined. We do not try different options and we are loath to see the choices that might exist – especially if these choices lead us into uncharted territory. It is not uncommon for us to default to finding our next steps by doing what is familiar, what we have always done. That tends to work well enough, until it does not. If we are unable to shift our perspective, we always do what we have always done. But what we have done in the past may not work in the present and might even be less effective for the future.

This default response applies to situations we face every day, whether at work or outside of work. At work, we build habits and practices, learn skills, build competencies, gain experience, and develop mastery around our usual tasks – whether we are a barista, call centre operator, opera singer, entrepreneur, or CEO. We seek comfort in habits that provide us with answers to our questions, as most of us prefer an answered question to an open question. Also, dealing with seemingly similar situations in similar ways by default is efficient; not a bad idea, after all. However, if we misinterpret the situation because we are not considering and approaching it from different perspectives, we might default to a highly efficient reaction that gives us an ineffective result. In short, we default to efficiently doing the wrong thing.

Taking perspective opens choices, it impacts the decisions that we make. How do we know if our decision is the best one for the moment? "Taking perspective" involves changing the perspective we already have and considering other one(s)[3]. Often, we conflate our perspective with reality. In addition, we often assume that our perspective is the same as others' perspectives. That assumption reveals a blindness that sometimes can create challenges or mischief. We may find, in hindsight and with more information, that the best decision in the moment may not have been the best decision, leading to the familiar phrase, "it sounded like a good idea at the time". In hindsight, of course, we are always smarter.

What happens if we don't "take perspective"?

If we don't take perspective, and follow our instincts instead, we use what we metaphorically call "autopilot". And that might be a good idea in many instances.

For example, you have a weekly report you draft and deliver to your manager on Fridays. You both agree what is needed, you use a template, you are on autopilot. Job done efficiently.

This suffices (satisfies your manager, has you operating efficiently) until circumstances change in a relevant and meaningful way. The change will cause your standard, automatic output to be insufficient. Or worse even, your autopilot has stopped you from thinking altogether. You need to choose a different perspective to see what must now be done.

The more complex a situation – one that is different from what we have experienced – the more we will benefit from putting a pause between stimulus and response. By doing so, we allow a broader set of perspectives to emerge. We allow ourselves to create options and make choices based on thoughtful reflection. We create the time and space to think, and to question or consult with others, tapping into their knowledge and experience and using their advice as input for our reflection. Creating this space and time gives us the possibility to exercise choice, to use various perspectives, or to shift perspectives.

In our earlier story, by using additional cameras and shifting our perspective, we are now able to make sense differently – to see a good Samaritan rather than a skinhead attack. Our pathway forward will be different vs. our default autopilot defined by one narrow perspective.

The theoretical foundation of this concept has greatly benefited from the work of Daniel Kahneman and Amos Tversky, most prominently published in *Thinking Fast, Thinking Slow*[4]. "Thinking fast" is what we refer to as autopilot; "thinking slow" is what happens during and after reflection and perspective-taking. The following describes in some practical detail what it looks like when we move from the autopilot steering us to making deliberate choices based on carefully using information provided by conscious cognitive processes.

Three questions will help us unpack this evolution from autopilot to deliberate choices based on different perspectives, building a robust understanding of what is possible:

- "What can we do to enhance our ability to take perspectives?"
- "How can we engage in perspective-taking?"
- "What can get in the way?"

What can we do to enhance our ability to take perspectives?

Enhancing perspective-taking requires putting a pause between stimulus and response (which is greatly helped by being in a state of mindfulness, as described in our chapter on mindfulness). The more we are willing and able to pause before responding (to the extent that the situation allows), the more we open the options space and give ourselves room to make conscious choices. As Viktor Frankl explained: "Between stimulus and response there is a space. In that space is our power to choose our response. In our response lies our growth and our freedom."

Neurologically, unfortunately, we cannot lengthen this pause[5], which is less than a second (think of how fast you might react after you feel a mosquito sting in your arm, or how you react when behind the wheel of your car you see a ball rolling onto the street just ahead of you). If we let ourselves be subordinated to our neurological limits, we lose the capacity to consciously pause, reflect, see options, and make use of available choices. If we let our reflexes take the wheel, we may end up feeling like a victim after doing something that, upon scrutiny, seems to be the second choice at best. Only if we find a way to notice and elongate the pause can conscious thinking start, giving us the space to develop options. We might have to ignore what our physiology wants us to do. We must find the time and calm to notice our own inner impulse and take a deep breath – to interrupt the automaticity of the connection between the stimulus and the response. Otherwise, we merely react, without any real opportunity to do something different from what we have done in the past.

Carol Kauffman suggests a beautifully simple way of putting that pause between stimulus and response. She invites us to ask ourselves:

"Who do I want to *be* right now?"[6].

If we allow this question to work its way into our system (head, heart, gut, or wherever we process this type of question), we have already created the pause.

Notice how this question is different from the usual question, "What can I/we *do* right now?"

Being is richer than *doing*[7], and is also one step removed from action (doing) as it allows the space for a second question (once the "Who do I want to be right now?" has been answered): "And what am I going to do now to be who I want to be?"

Let's take an example. As we drive on a country road, we see a few cars sitting by the roadside; apparently there has been an accident. Multiple people stand outside of their cars around the scene of the accident. What next? The "being" question could be something like, "Who do I want to be in this situation?". If we choose to say "a curious bystander", or "an observer", the number of "doing" options is rather limited: We might slow down, watch the situation to satisfy our basic need for curiosity, then accelerate again and continue our journey as if nothing had happened – but at least we know that we have a story to tell later in the day.

Choosing the other option, "engaged", however, opens the option space. We can stop our car, get out, and ask people whether we can help. The options could range from satisfying our curiosity to lending a hand to offering help by bringing our specialist skills to bear (e.g., if someone is severely injured and we know what needs to be done before the ambulance arrives).

We can also just take a deep breath (counting "21, 22, 23" while inhaling, then exhaling) and start practicing *calm*, one of the 5 C's that Douglas Choo describes in his article, *A leader's resilience: Not as intuitive as you think*[8] (and that we also refer to in the chapter on mindfulness).

Calm means that we can reduce any spontaneous energy from a situation. We can reduce the arousal of our entire system (head, heart, gut) from the stimulus. Calm allows us to realize even in a situation that generates fear, such as speaking in front of a large audience, we are not dealing with a sabre-toothed tiger. Once calm is achieved, we can then use the next C, *curiosity*. We can ask, "What could be the motives of the other person for saying what they say, for doing what they do?" Or we can ask, "How can I help?". Curiosity is at the start of most – if not all – important discoveries of humankind. Sir Isaac Newton is famous for wondering why the apple fell from the tree – as opposed to just picking up the apple and eating it. Had he not been curious, our world would be different now. Or someone else would have made Newton's discovery instead.

How can we engage in perspective-taking?

Perspective-taking is a habit that works like a muscle: If we don't regularly practice perspective-taking, it will lose its strength. If, on the other hand, we regularly practice perspective-taking, then over time our muscle memory will kick in; perspective-taking will then become intuitive and more automatic, functioning without any deliberate effort on our part. The following are some steps we can take to help us practice perspective-taking.

Look around. One thing we can do is simply look around us. If you are like most adults, you look tall when standing next to a first grader. When standing next to LeBron James, however, you are not tall. But you are still the same height. This is the most basic version of looking around us: comparing ourselves to the physical space we are in.

Zoom in and out: Zooming in and out (as with a good camera) is about our ability to direct our attention to the big picture and to focus on selected aspects of a situation or a person, appreciating the contribution of those details, positive or negative. Think of a visit to a museum with paintings by old masters, perhaps Turners or Rembrandts or van Goghs. When we stand very close to a painting, we notice details that explain their mastery, e.g., how they paint the face of a woman or a flower in full blossom. When we move a little further away, we see the same face in the context of the whole picture, and the meaning might change from "a beautiful woman" to "a witness of the coronation of a queen". We might wonder how this woman might have experienced the coronation and what might have brought her there, and where and how she lived. When we move even further away, to the middle of the room where we sit down on a beautiful Barcelona chair, we can look at the same painting and see how it compares to the other five paintings in the same room – paintings by different painters telling different stories. Now we might ask ourselves, "Had I had the opportunity to be a personal witness of any of the moments shown in these paintings, which one would I have preferred?" See how the different vantage points we take give us a range of perspectives of a single painting?

This "zooming in and out" can also happen in a different form. For example, we might like or even admire people despite their known and visible shortcomings. Instead of zooming in on their shortcomings, we zoom out and appreciate their general, positive attributes. For example, an extremely assertive leader might be an advantage to a team that is lost and stressed.

"Zooming in and out" also is at the heart of one of the most often-used images in leadership, an image we owe to Ronald Heifetz[9]: getting off the dance floor and onto the balcony. This analogy posits that our experience of what is happening on the dance floor is very different depending on whether we're positioned right inside the action or overlooking it. The "balcony" allows us to take a step back and reflect on what we see from this different perspective – which leads to a richer understanding of a situation.

Time: There is a less visceral, more conceptual way of taking perspective: along the flow of time. We can compare ourselves to an earlier version of ourselves and be happy or unhappy about what we have achieved, how we have grown, and/or what we have learned. We might also be able to project ourselves into the future and develop a future version of ourselves, perhaps even an ideal version of ourselves, make the comparison with who and where we are today, and derive energy from the idea of closing the gap.

The ability to access these different perspectives depends on our perceptual apparatus (our eyes, ears, and other related senses, as well as our cognitive flexibility), on our willingness to accept and work around biases (of which there are many, as we will see later in the chapter), on our willingness and ability to let go of our ego (as in "my way or the highway"), and on our ability to create enough calm to be able to see the forest for the trees.

Values: Our values, that is, what is most important to us, are important filters for all of us. They can be used to gauge what is acceptable to us and what is not. How much are we willing to flex our own perspective when we meet others with different values? And what if this clash of values involves hierarchies – e.g., we believe camaraderie is important, but our boss does not?

Priorities: What is important to us *now*? That is the key question, one that is simple but not asked often enough. A sound understanding of our priorities gives us a good idea of what we should pay attention to, which cues to follow and which to ignore. And the notion of priorities allows for added flexibility – priorities might change over time as some events become more imminent or more important than others, which will have an impact on our ability and willingness to take perspective. After changing his mind on a major policy issue, Konrad Adenauer, the first chancellor of the post-war Federal Republic of Germany, was asked by a journalist why he had changed his mind, suggesting that he could no longer be seen as reliable. His reply: "No one can prevent me from becoming smarter overnight."

Scenarios: "What if?" is a key question that can lead to the development of different perspectives. Scenarios enable us to take a variety of factors into consideration and then arrange them flexibly to create new perspectives on what's around or ahead of us. We can also explore what happens if we change just one element, everything else being equal.

The **"inner team"/"internal board of directors"**: Various researchers[9] have proposed variations of an idea that we might have an equivalent of an advisory board, but on a personal scale, inside of us. The multiple members of this internal team or board represent a broad set of perspectives and experiences that come together in support of our objectives and ambitions.

Think of the young professional who is offered what seems to be an interesting job in a different company. That young professional asks her "inner team" for advice on what to do. The courageous voice might say, "Go for it"; the cautious voice might say, "Hang on a minute, let's first find out about XYZ before making a decision"; the growth voice might say, "What a fantastic opportunity"; the community voice might say, "You cannot leave your current colleagues behind and let them down"; and the list goes on. Researchers suggest that if we imagine presenting our ideas for actions to this inner team or internal board of directors, we access the same wisdom as if we were consulting an actual advisory board in our professional reality.

The concept of the "inner theatre" takes this idea one step further, combining it with the dance floor/balcony image proposed by Ronald Heifetz. This inner theatre concept gives us the option of mentally acting out a play on stage using various characters. The inner play includes a director, technicians, and an audience. In our minds, we can rehearse, and even do a dress rehearsal, which leads, of course, to the show itself. We can explore the different perspectives of the individuals involved (actors, directors, audience members, etc.) by asking: "What does it look and feel like to see/be this character in this play?".

We can then learn by carefully listening to and combining the answers.

Another way of looking at this internal team or internal board of directors' concept is through the lens of the "Internal Family Systems" model by Richard Schwartz[10]. Schwartz talks about the different parts or voices inside of us who have different opinions on various situations. It's a far more elaborate and grounded version of the more colloquial visual that we sometimes use of the little angel sitting on one shoulder and the little devil sitting on the other, both commenting on events and suggesting different courses of action.

Now that we have discussed how to enhance your ability to do perspective-taking and how to actually do it, let's talk about what might cloud your perspective. What might get in the way?

What can get in the way?

Despite our best intentions to approach situations from different perspectives, our efforts may be hampered by psychological or emotional barriers. This section lists a few of those barriers.

Biases and Filters: First and foremost, we must look at biases and filters. We begin with unconscious bias, on which much has been written.

The topic of unconscious bias is a highly important one that profoundly impacts perspective. Generally speaking, increasing inner and outer awareness (see the chapter on mindfulness) is one of the key tactics we can use to pull bias from the realm of the unconscious to our conscious awareness. The first step in surfacing unconscious bias is to accept that to be human is to have unconscious biases embedded in our survival imperative. We unconsciously ignore information that seems to be inconsistent or threatening to our quest.

Indeed, Margaret Heffernan takes it further. In her wonderful book *Wilful Blindness*[11], she argues that we can choose to see or hear something[12], to start to be aware of something, and still turn a blind eye on that very information when it comes to making sense of a situation. Think of your pet project. There might be voices of support and voices against. Willful blindness might lead to overestimating what's in favour – i.e., the one study that supports your idea – and to justify to yourself and others why the facts that speak against your idea – i.e., all the other studies – are not that convincing after all.

In addition to unconscious bias, obsolete filters can also hamper the effectiveness of our efforts to take perspective. Perhaps many of our filters are now obsolete given the new environment. Filters were built to help us deal with past formative events that we have stored as major experiences. While these situations have moved on, the filters have stayed. Too many people apply their filters from yesterday to situations of today and find they lack what's needed to deal with the newer situations. The results vary from just missing the mark to being grossly and utterly wrong.

The faster our situations change or the greater the complexity of these changes, the higher the risk that the practices we have adopted as effective will not serve us well, as the past is no longer a good predictor of the future. The risk, plainly speaking, is that we have not adjusted our filters sufficiently, with the result that we disregard information that was not important back then but is important now. We end up looking at the wrong data, making insufficient evaluations, and missing the opportunity to move closer to our goals.

Assumptions: Assumptions are a special form of filters that we all use. Consultants are taught to ask as many questions as possible to obtain as much information as possible so they can make good, data-based recommendations. However, there may not be enough time to ask all the questions, or key people are not available, or – worse – are unwilling to answer their questions. In such situations, consultants will turn to working with assumptions. They then create a compelling concept to solve the client's issue at hand, and package it up in a nice deck only to discover during the presentation that they have missed the mark. Their assumptions, it seems, were inadequate, and thus the opportunity to have critical questions answered passes. Work with assumptions if needed but replace them as early as possible with real answers to real questions. The alternative is to run the risk of your assumptions being incomplete or outdated or overtaken by events, which may result in inadequately dealing with situations at hand – and inadequate approaches seldom yield strong and positive results.

Overload: We often find ourselves in a phase of overload, cognitive or otherwise, when we constantly have more on our plate than we can digest. In this situation, we find it hard to give ourselves permission to slow down to access the state of "calm" we described earlier in this chapter. The more pressure we feel, the more difficult it becomes to calm down, and the higher the risk that our focus will narrow to the point where we no longer can see what might be of crucial importance. We also "pull up the bridges", increasing the sensitivity of our filters to let less (potentially important) information pass through, as seen during the recent pandemic. To make matters worse, most of us find it terrifyingly difficult to say "no" to new requests, being afraid of being seen as not sufficiently high performing or letting our friends or colleagues down.

Misinterpreting the cues: Sometimes we narrow our filters and pull up the bridges when we erroneously believe we are under enormous pressure. We don't always read the available cues correctly. As a result, we feel under pressure, with limited options, when in reality we have more time on our hands and could calm down first before jumping to action. Some of these mistaken interpretations of cues may be connected to a rush of anxiety, fatigue, or even peer pressure.

Fear: As the actor Will Smith eloquently explains: "Fear is not real. It is a product of thoughts you create. Do not misunderstand me. Danger is very real. But fear is a choice." Or, to use the words of George Addair: "Everything you've ever wanted is on the other side of fear." We all experience fear from time to time; it is one of the most normal of human reactions. Perhaps we do not have the courage to experiment, or we may be overwhelmed by the amount of information coming at us. Emotions then take over, and we find it increasingly hard to access our rational, logical ability to process. Before we can regroup and decide to properly see the options, autopilot kicks in with a warning: "If you are afraid of the answer, don't ask the question." Before we know it, the opportunity to be courageous has dissipated.

Think back to the story at the start of this chapter, as the facilitator faced a group of frustrated, angry leaders on the edge of mutiny. After letting the leaders vent their frustration with Mike, their boss, the facilitator had the courage to ask, "Now tell me what you like about Mike". This courageous question unleashed a flow of positive comments about Mark, revealing to the leaders a different perspective they barely knew existed.

Role and power: For various reasons, we may feel we are not entitled to voicing our opinion or we may not have the courage to offer different perspectives[13]. Perhaps we are "the new kid on the block" in the team ("how can you know, having come for a different industry/function/part of the business?"). Perhaps we are in a minority position due to tenure, gender, or any other criterion that might be visible or relevant in the situation. Or perhaps we have to battle groupthink and peer pressure ("come on, don't be a bore") that deride what is important to us ("and here comes Joe again with his 'values' thing").

In some cases, our roles may hamper perspective-taking because of conflicting priorities and pressures. An SVP of supply chain management I worked with many years ago explained the conundrum of his role as follows: the SVP of manufacturing asks him to predict as exactly as possible the quantities of each of the products to be produced over the next three months (and he can do that); the SVP of sales asks him to ensure that the business is able to supply each product to each client in the desired quantity within 48 hours, globally (and he can do that); the CFO asks him to reduce inventory to the strict minimum (and he can do that). However, he cannot do all three at the same time. He understands the different perspectives of his three colleagues, but do they understand *his* dilemma?

There's yet another element of role that can hamper perspective-taking. Imagine we are the leader of a struggling business. Eventually, we realize it is time to lay off some of our employees. One of them has our gender identity, is about the same age, has kids as we do, and may even live in the same part of town. From our personal perspective, we might struggle to make and communicate the decision to let this person go; while from our business perspective, it is the only sensible decision ... we can easily imagine the inner conflict brought about by these two very visible perspectives connected to each of our roles (executive vs. parent).

Intercultural dimensions: Intercultural dimensions can lead to different perspectives that others may not be aware of. Perhaps we are operating in a learned language among native speakers, and our ability to express ourselves with the degree of nuance that we are used to is limited. Perhaps we have learned to wait to contribute until we are asked, while the culture we now operate in values assertiveness. Some of us may come from a culture that likes to be direct and communicate in a no-nonsense style, "calling a spade a spade", while others think that such directness is rude beyond repair as they value an indirect, highly descriptive communications style. Finally, if you work globally, you will certainly have come across virtual meetings that have participants from 6 or more time zones, leading to different perspectives on the chosen meeting time. If the meeting is from 8 – 10 am for you (comfortable for most), that translates to 5 – 7 am for others. An early afternoon meeting, say from 1 – 3 pm for you (again comfortable for most) is from 7 – 9 pm for other participants. If these discrepancies happen repeatedly, those who hold the wrong end of the stick will be limited in their ability, and later willingness, to contribute to the meeting.

Ignoring intercultural dimensions not only leads to inconvenience for certain people; it can lead to others questioning our values. When we blur or reduce our perspective by blocking out what is not important to us, and add a dose of willful blindness, we can become ignorant of what should be important. For example, the average workday in Tokyo starts before the average workday in Mumbai, then Berlin, then London, and New York City or Boston hours later. When the average workday has long ended in Tokyo, it has not even started in Los Angeles or San Francisco. Imagine you live in the Central European Time (CET) time zone, 6 hours "ahead" of Eastern Time in the US. Your average workday then overlaps with Tokyo, with Mumbai, and with the US East Coast. A slightly longer average workday even overlaps with the US West Coast. These overlaps are highly visible for everyone in the CET time zone but can easily slip through the filters of those who live in Tokyo or on the US East Coast. What is completely and easily evident for some of us quite often gets unconsciously ignored by others. And when this happens repeatedly, we will find ourselves wondering what it would take for someone else, beyond some good will, to realize what is important and evident to others – to "stand in their shoes". This realization leads quickly to the impression that "my situation is not important for you", which just as quickly turns into "I am not important to you". If this happens, a simple act of not standing in someone else's shoes could cause a values conflict, as it subtly says, "Your point of view does not interest me," which translates into "What is important for you is not important for me."

One situation that brings it all together nicely: your next 360-degree feedback

We finish this chapter with a highly practical example that many leaders have experienced: 360-degree feedback, almost the embodiment of "perspective taking" in conjunction with stakeholder perspectives. If conducted properly, in a corporate culture that is reasonably open to feedback and development and knows how to keep things confidential, there is no better collection of cues for perspective taking than a 360-degree feedback. The blend of useful perspectives provided by the diverse participants in the 360-degree feedback process sits right there before our eyes.

The feedback reflects how others perceive us, how they describe what they see or experience in our company, and what impact our behaviour has on them.

This feedback is coloured by the position, relative to ours, of those offering the feedback: boss, superior, peer, direct report, other. Changes in the relationship can also influence the feedback. Unsurprisingly, one of the most demanding transitions for leaders is that from peer in a team to leader of the same team, where someone who was a peer yesterday is now a direct report.

To ensure the effectiveness of the different perspectives received through 360-degree feedback, we can ask several questions. What is the quality of interaction that we have with those giving the feedback: do we partner most of the time, do we depend upon one another, do we compete for resources? How much can we be ourselves in these interactions, aligning what we do with who we are (e.g., being authentic)? Do we have to play a role for the sake of some greater good or because our boss has asked us to? Do we find ourselves in a shadow conflict because our bosses hate each other, and we must play along and be loyal to our respective bosses?

How often do we interact with one another? How many data points do we have and use? How long are these interactions? How savvy is everyone involved when it comes to technology used to make these interactions happen?

Who does the other person remind us of? Who do we remind them of? What do we project onto them? And they onto us?

How willing are we to "just play along in the exercise," or how courageous are we to say, "Ok, I will play along, and I will also seek to speak with someone I have provided feedback to so that they hear what I really have to say and what I absolutely want them to be aware of."

How does the current situation in the firm influence the exercise? A firm that has enjoyed good growth rates and strong results probably has less conflicts "under the hood" than a firm that is in dire straits, where the available cake is no longer large enough to feed everyone.

The list of potential questions continues, but you get the idea. All these perspectives are likely to colour the outcome and have an impact on how people lead, cooperate, and achieve results effectively and efficiently.

Key Take-Aways from this Chapter

We mentioned earlier in this chapter the notion of muscle memory, the ability of the body to remember specific movements that are the result of repeated practice. Ask anyone who plays golf or tennis, for example, and you will quickly hear them speak about this phenomenon.

Something equivalent to physical muscle memory exists to underpin our ability to take on different perspectives before we come to conclusions, make decisions, and act. The following questions will help us practice better perspective-taking (this is just a starting point, you will certainly add your preferred questions as well):

1. How can I best create a pause between stimulus and response?

2. Who do I want to **be** right now?

3. What do I notice when I scan the environment/look around me?

4. What are the key details, and what is the big picture?

5. How does this compare to this time last year/two years ago/three years ago?

6. What is important to me now?

7. What do I want others to think of me?

8. How do I filter what I notice, how am I biased?

9. How do I filter the relevant information and separate it from the noise around it?

10. How does my bias serve me?

11. What am I afraid of?

12. How does my fear serve me? What if I were not afraid?

13. What are my key assumptions?

14. Whose view is important?

15. What could I **do** right now, what are the options?

We will dive deeper into some of these questions in the following chapters. In the meantime, asking yourself at least some of these questions before making important decisions will broaden your horizon and deepen your insight, which, in turn, will allow for richer perspectives and better decisions.

CHAPTER 5

"R" is for Reality

Donna ran Human Resources at one of her company's U.S. locations. She was promoted because she was passionate about what the function could do for employees, and had skills aligned with the role. Her job was to handle compensation and benefits, as well as to ensure proper policies and procedures were in place and being followed. During her first year in the job, many of her performance metrics trended towards meeting or exceeding expectations. *What* she was focusing on was appropriate. However, there were also complaints to the Vice President Global Talent (her manager) about *how* Donna was doing her role.

When she was offered (and accepted) a chance to receive leadership coaching, she already recognized that she had an issue worth addressing[1]. She knew that something was not working well, even if she could not yet identify the cause nor what to do about it. When we looked closer at the complaints, Donna seemed to be rigid, insensitive, and authoritarian about how she approached fellow employees' issues. In fact, several described her style as punitive parental.

This led to an exploration of Donna's home environment. A single parent with a young child, Donna also had a younger sister who lived with them until tragedy struck: her sister was killed in a home invasion three years earlier. Donna was doing her best to deal with the loss; this included seeing a therapist to work through her grief, feelings of guilt, and fear about being able to protect her daughter. She was hypervigilant and somewhat defensive at home and brought that same perspective and attitude to work.

In both contexts, she intended the best for those she was serving. However, there were consequences to the way she was interacting with others at work. She was emotionally raw and subject to overreaction. Though she could hear and understand employees' stated concerns, it was difficult for her to empathize, connect, listen well, and problem solve without dictating solutions. According to her, she was simply trying to take care of her internal clients.

When Donna was able to take a step back and look at how she was thinking, feeling, and behaving at home and at work, she could see the connection and similarity between the two locations. She could see that she was bringing the same mindset and practices from working with her child to working with her clients – a pattern she recognized as inappropriate and ineffective. She wondered whether, with professional support, she could make some desired improvements.

Her starting point was noticing where she was at the moment. What was true about right here, right now? How did it differ from where she wanted and intended to be? Analyzing the data, making sense of the gap between where she was and where she wanted to be, and identifying root causes suggested how to intervene and what to adjust. She was an able problem-solver. With guidance and persistence, she could close gaps and blend (connect, orient, appreciate) better with her customers. We shall revisit her learning journey at the end of the chapter to see what happened.

Context

A map in a shopping mall (remember them?) indicates with an "X" where you are relative to stores and other amenities. It even labels your location with the bold statement, "You are here." Depending on where you want to go or what you want to accomplish, you can chart a path to your destination.

In the organizational world of formulating strategy, solving problems, and making decisions, pinpointing the "We are here" location is complex and depends in large part on what elements we use as our points of reference. Which facts are relevant? What time frame? Whose perspective?

The answers to these questions depend on where we want to go or what problem we are trying to solve. We have our habitual or traditional way of working through issues and challenges but sometimes, our automatic approach does not (or is unlikely to) get the job done well. What then? To accomplish excellent work, we must set out on a different journey, one that will help us to understand our reality, one requiring more thoughtfulness and mindfulness.

Here's an example of that situation

Derrick, SVP Business Development (BD) for a financial services company, had been in his role for eight years. Formerly a successful salesperson in the industry, he was promoted to organize and empower his organization. In the previous year, BD accounted for 95% of the sales generated by the business. Nevertheless, he had identified problems and was attempting to get them sorted out.

Still struggling with making the transition from individual contributor to manager, Derrick tended to do things himself rather than delegate. This extended to taking over the hiring process for senior-level client executives, ignoring the process already in place. In the past two years, he had hired three senior sales executives. Two of them were already failing; the third was only marginally successful. Their poor performance was creating pressure on other sales executives and fostering resentment. When asked on what basis he had made those hiring decisions, he replied that it was predominantly his assessment of how closely they resembled him and his positive characteristics.

This situation, and Derrick's difficulty in resolving it, was one of the reasons I was asked to provide leadership coaching. In fact, there were several issues for him to address: improve the performance of or fire the two underperforming sales executives; determine a different way to make strategic hires; and make the transition to acting like a manager.

To move towards a better future state, each issue required him to clearly see where he was at that moment – his current reality. Now was not a time for opinions, let alone confusing opinions for facts. To do a good job would demand knowing what facts were likely to be important and relevant, collecting them, and making sense of them. Achieving this goal raised a few questions worth considering:

- Whose perspectives (his and who else's) and history were important and worth including?
- What biases were operating?
- Did the data include only observable behaviour or feelings and assessments as well?
- What assumptions were in play and were they grounded?
- What was the context and how was it similar or different from before?

Let's take a closer look at each of these areas.

Perspectives (POV) and History

Do I use my own perspective to understand where we are now? Who else should I tap for their data? People in my organization? Research and professional resources? All of the above?

The answer is indeed, "All of the above".

As situations migrate from complicated to complex, the need for multiple perspectives expands. No one person can understand a situation with all of its nuances. In fact, deeper understanding is likely to come from listening to others who have a diverse experiential basis for their facts. Others in our organization (for example, the CEO or the VP Human Resources) are different observers to our situation; they almost certainly see/hear different experiences that could be relevant for creating a fuller picture.

Another avenue to new perspectives is current research on the issue at hand. There also may be formal research conducted on a relevant question or less rigorous but still informative popular press articles that appear in the business literature which offer different perspectives and interpretations. These may be worth tracking down, reviewing, and considering.

In the above case, Derrick drew on his own experience and understanding of the client executives' past and current performance. He asked himself these questions:

- On what basis had he selected and hired these client executives?

- Why did he ignore the process in place?

- Why did he ignore the standards used in the process?

- How had he set expectations with them?

- How had he followed up?
- What feedback had he given?
- What had he done to correct, support, and improve their performance?

Through these questions, he discovered that he went with what he knew as an approach – *when in doubt, do it yourself.* This bias (see the following section) blinded him to seeking available and useful resources or even challenging his old practice. Since he had hired junior staff by using his own strengths as the template, he assumed that they would be equally applicable when hiring senior client executives. Because he did not have managers, let alone competent managers, in place at the time who could offer their perspectives, he was not aware that he could look beyond his "do it yourself" bias to be curious about how HR had set up their process, standards, and success criteria.

Once the senior client executives were hired, the quality of their sales work seemed to decline steadily, and Derrick's management of their promises suffered as well. While he had set goals and discussed his expectations with the sales executives, he had not given specific, timely feedback about their ongoing performance, had not documented incidents of poor planning or performance, had not discussed or implemented performance improvement plans, and had procrastinated in taking action to correct performance or terminate employment. He had avoided discussing the issues with HR and only obliquely responded to queries from the CEO. Such behaviour was noticed.

With coaching, Derrick acquired a different perspective of his situation and his contribution to the current state. He saw that to make things better, he would have to think and act differently, overcoming his embarrassment about his inaction and procrastination.

Positive steps included talking to the VP HR to learn more about the hiring process currently in place in the company. She shared the selection methodology and criteria for making an informed decision (which were significantly different from, and more robust and evidence-based, than what Derrick used). He also talked to the CEO to get his observations and assessments about the client executives. In total, he now had access to six different perspectives and histories related to his situation. He also received several articles on the importance of using proven hiring procedures and the role of effective hiring practices in beginning a virtuous life cycle of a productive employee. He could now see that the "reality" that he was facing had been due largely to poor hiring practices.

Biases

As human beings, we are prone to make judgments and choices influenced by our cognitive, often unconscious, biases. Without self-awareness, most of our biases will remain unconscious. Without mindfulness, too, we may not be able to interrupt ourselves and question whether we are observing a situation clearly and thinking objectively about it.

When we solve problems, it's likely that some of our biases are in play, affecting the process and potentially skewing our deliberations and decisions. They may constrain where we look for information, what we find credible, or even the kinds of decisions to consider legitimate or viable. They are likely to influence our assumptions as well (as shown in the assumptions section below). It seems that biases and assumptions are intimately connected.

There are entire courses designed to help us identify our biases (especially unconscious ones) and their associated assumptions, and thus help us develop new practices. According to Rewire[2], here are several actions we can take to identify and shift our own biases:

- exercise mindfulness to pause and question whether biases are in play;
- be curious about what may be influencing our decisions;
- examine who might be impacted by our action and what form that would take;
- choose to slow down and seek additional data;
- seek other, reliable sources for their points of view; and
- think about our own history with similar situations and the decisions we made then.

In Derrick's case and with open-ended questions, he began to see what biases were operating and what he could do to either shift them or take them into account. For example, once he identified his bias of "doing it his (old) way", he could make a different, conscious choice to widen the frame and include other approaches. His bias of "hire others like me", already challenged by client executives' poor performance, caused him to question what might be a more effective protocol to apply when selecting candidates. In turn, this had him talking with internal experts – the HR folks – about what they did and why. Another of his biases (and associated assumption) was that "telling people one time about something important should be sufficient." Challenging this bias enabled him to see that effective management required multiple communications and a structure to help others recognize what is important and a priority.

Kinds of data

The easiest kind of reality to identify is observable – what we perceive with our senses. Beyond that, and depending on who the observer is, the data become more subjective and inaccessible to social verification. That does not mean, however, that such data should be ignored, but rather simply understood in context.

Observable data include the kinds of things counted in organizations: time spent, behaviours observed, results of various kinds, noted at a moment in time or over time (such as trends). For example, a hospital system had a project to develop a new, web-based collaboration platform for information sharing across many different stakeholders. It used the experiences of several organizations thought to have best practices in similar situations. These provided relevant methods for consideration, along with associated data and evaluations of their results.

Non-observable data include the things we can only access by asking others to report on their experiences. This reflects others' affect (feeling state), interpretations of their experiences and judgments about that person or experience. This is the case when data is gathered in a 360° interview or survey process. The intent is to gather others' perceptions (understood as perceptions) about the client.

For Derrick, he had both observable and non-observable data about his failing client executives. He had their observed behaviours and the results of those behaviours, as well as his own behaviours with them and with the CEO.

He also had his own affect (frustration, disappointment, embarrassment) and his own interpretations and stories about these individuals and their performance. In addition, he also had others' interpretations and stories about his own performance through our debriefing of his 360° interview data.

The data allowed Derrick to observe how he had been operating as both an observer and an actor in the world. He recognized how he was making sense of the data and how his assumptions (see following section) shaped his actions and what he saw as possible. Through reflection invited by open-ended questions, he could see additional interpretations as available to him. These additional interpretations would lead, in turn, to different implications and choices. His range of mindful actions increased as his horizon of possibilities expanded. His own affect shifted to curiosity and ambition, energizing a fresh approach to his situation.

Assumptions

We cannot get away from making assumptions. They allow us to make sense of our world more efficiently, better predict the future, and increase our likelihood of survival. On the other hand, if we generate less effective assumptions, we constrain ourselves and our ability to navigate our world well. This happens when our circumstances change, especially rapidly, as is the case in VUCA context. Assumptions and associated practices well-fitted to prior and current conditions can become ill-fitted to a new environment. As Marshall Goldsmith[3] wryly observed about the conundrum of promotions, "What got you here won't get you there."

Assumptions are also connected to expectations. They seem to go in pairs. Often the expectation is couched in "should" terms: "They should do this," "She ought to be that way," and so on. The dangerous part of this dynamic duo of assumption/expectation is that they are often invisible to us, while being profoundly impactful on others. If we are blind to our assumptions (and associated expectations), then we are unable to recognize, discuss, negotiate, alter, or realign them to fit the reality. In short, we are unable to make the most of them.

We must make the most of our assumptions because assumptions are an unavoidable part of our lives. There are two moves we can make to give us a better set of assumptions to work with. Both require mindfulness and self-awareness, which enable us to reflect on our thought process and identify assumptions that shape our perceptions and choices. A coaching conversation is one way to trigger such a reflection.

The first move is to adjust or refine our assumptions. For example, can we learn where and in what ways to adjust our assumptions to better fit our facts? Sometimes an assumptive tweak is sufficient to enable effective action.

While working with severely disabled children and their families, my assessment of "no client progress" was based on an assumption of how much and how persistent the behavioural changes needed to be as evidence of progress. As pointed out to me by the program director, I was using standards for an able-bodied population, not this one. His statement enabled me to adjust my assumption to be appropriate to the group I was working with. As a result, I figuratively had "fresh eyes" to observe the impact of our work. I could draw different conclusions, remaining resilient in the face of smaller change increments and less persistent progress than originally expected.

Another example of adjusting an assumption is to assume that every challenging situation is a problem to solve. This framing automatically leads us to look for specific kinds of resolutions (e.g., simple solutions) while being blind to other opportunities. Some situations are more complicated or even complex and require several integrated solutions. Others, because they have opposing, interdependent answers (e.g., task vs. relationship) require dynamically managing the polarities without seeking a single, right answer[4]. Finally, some challenging situations have no solutions at all; they are mysteries that we invite to our inquiry[5]. Adjusting our assumptions to more nuanced situations will lead us to better diagnoses and more effective responses.

The second move is to identify which assumptions to drop and which new ones to acquire. Because assumptions are always contextualized (though we often are oblivious of this as shown in the following section), their usefulness is contingent on remaining tightly coupled to the current environment. When conditions change, the coupling can loosen, and the intended efficiency of working with assumptions decreases. It's time to take stock and take action. What old assumptions are worth discarding completely because they no longer fit? And what new assumptions should we rely on to streamline our cognitive processes?

For example, given an opportunity to thoughtfully design a path towards a desired future, clients often drop their assumption of being a *victim* of circumstances, replacing it with the assumption of being a *player*, someone who believes "I have the resources to find a way"[6]. Many people have also recognized and dropped the assumption of having to be "perfect", while still maintaining high standards.

Derrick, like many of us, had made many assumptions

when conducting his business and his life. Regarding his management style, he assumed that others were just like him: self-starting, highly motivated, considerate, interested in playing a collaborative team game, and a lifelong learner. In fact, they were not like him, and that was an assumption to discard. Similarly, he assumed he could do as good a job (if not better) as HR in hiring sales staff. Partially true at best. He also assumed people only needed to be told something once, which would be sufficient to get the job done. False, and another assumption to cast aside.

One new assumption Derrick began to make was that "leaders bring the weather." In other words, leaders are responsible for the emotional tone (mood) they embody when engaging with their staff. That tone is contagious, for better or for worse.

Finally, one assumption, that all sales executives could be evaluated according to the same criteria, only needed adjusting. Having made some bad decisions based on that flawed assumption, Derrick refined it to refer only to junior sales staff. For senior positions, he recognized that he needed the perspective and expertise of others.

Context

Context is a part of every current state and it differs for each of us. Our "context" is the background from which we observe ourselves, others, and the world. Our context is based on our history and personal narratives. Therefore, context influences our interpretation of our environment, where we fit, and what is possible.

Among the many distinct lenses through which to view one's context, here are three to be curious about:

- purpose/intention

- culture/psychological safety

- mindset

Purpose can be viewed as the big brother of (superordinate to) intention. It's the answer to the question 'why?' Organizationally, it is why we exist, it is the way we add value and make the world a better place. Purpose is also why we exist on a personal level; it is our answer to ourselves of what we are here on earth to manifest. Everything can be viewed through the lens of purpose and understood in terms of organizing and acting consistently with that purpose. Consider it our north star. Businesses that are purpose-driven tend to be more successful than others[7].

Intention serves a similar organizing principle, but on a smaller, more intimate, operational scale. It can speak to what we intend for an interaction (e.g., a conversation or meeting) and guide our self-managing behaviours.

Culture is about the often unspoken but operative beliefs, values, assumptions, behaviours, and norms that characterize an identified group[8]. We often do not recognize our own culture until we travel to another one and discover meaningful differences, as well as similarities. This is a common experience in the workplace as well as in everyday life. When we move from one organization to another (or even one function to another within the same organization), we may find the (sub)cultures different, requiring adjustments (acculturation) on our part.

According to Schein[9], there are three distinct levels of organizational culture: its artifacts and practices, espoused values, and basic assumptions. Each level contributes something to the reality that must be recognized, understood, and effectively navigated.

Artifacts and practices include the architecture, design of the physical space, dress code, policies, procedures, language, and traditional ways of operating – "how we do things around here". They provide guidance about how to behave to be part of the group. The employees also serve as an organization's brand ambassadors to the outside world.

Espoused values reflect needs, rules of behaviour, and priorities. Mission, vision, and goals represent what is important. They reflect public-facing statements of philosophy and identity, projecting what the organization hopes to become. Senior managers need to model (act consistently with) those values rather than simply proclaim them. Sometimes there is a difference between the values that are spoken about and the implied values drawn from tacit, underlying assumptions. This misalignment can be the cause for miscommunication, miscoordination, and waste in performance.

Cultural assumptions are the foundational premise for the organization. Deeply embedded, usually unconscious, and well integrated into work behaviours, they are recognizable in everyone's actions.

Psychological safety is a group phenomenon that can occur within a culture or subculture. It reflects the assessment that it is safe to raise difficult, risky, or controversial issues without fear of being shut down or punished[10]. It was found to be the primary characteristic of high-performing teams at Google[11] and is best modelled and initially fostered by the team leader. There are specific behaviours a leader can engage in that contribute to producing psychological safety[12].

Mindset has to do with our orientation to life experiences, an established set of attitudes reflecting how we think about things and judge ourselves, and the implications of that perspective[13]. Individuals with a "fixed mindset" frame experiences in terms of their fixed talents and capabilities and have a judgment about their sufficiency; challenges are to be avoided. Individuals with a "growth mindset" frame their current capabilities as a work in progress. Further growth and learning are possible, desirable, and can be intentionally designed into their lives. This optimistic attitude is one of the influential contributing competencies of emotional self-regulation[14]. What's most important is that those attitudes need not be set. One can learn to develop a growth mindset and experience life and its range of choices differently.

Derrick, of course, was operating inside his own context. An aspect of his context was his growth mindset. Though not enthusiastic about the coaching engagement initially, he warmed to the opportunity and welcomed being challenged. One conversation that resonated with him was that of framing new perspectives and behaviours as an *experiment* to run[15].

Consistent with the work on complex contexts[16], the primary intent of an experiment is to learn, not to get it right or produce desired results. Derrick found that perspective liberating, providing freedom to play without attachment and the freedom to learn with curiosity. This fuelled a new, non-defensive conversation with HR to discuss how he could think and act differently in his hiring practices. This would pay dividends in designing a better process.

Experimentation also played a role in his intention setting. Derrick began to reflect on and articulate his intentions for the crucial conversations he would need to have with his failing sales executives. But first, he had to assess his options: was there a chance he could salvage either or both of the new executives with proper performance management? Guided by his intention to do good analysis and be informed by the result, he was able to determine the best course for all concerned: he let them go[17].

Although he did not experience psychological safety on the senior leadership team, Derrick was open to behaving in a way that encouraged a sense of psychological safety in his direct reports. Their psychological safety (or lack thereof) is their reality. Consistent with Edmondson's[18] recommendations, he began to behave differently to create a safer environment for all his people. Thus, when he decided to fire the two sales executives, he was able to have caring, respectful, and courageous conversations that left everyone feeling good despite any concerns the firings might have initially caused.

Derrick warmed to the idea of having managers he could lean on to manage his sales executives. To do so would require him to actively hire and/or develop sales executives to be managers. Intention in place, he began to groom three sales executives to take on a manager's role. Over time, he developed a strong group of managers who reduced his managerial burden and enabled him to take a more strategic approach to his function.

Returning to Donna

As Donna, whose story opened this chapter, began to increase her degree of self-awareness, she had new information to include and consider about how to improve her performance and satisfaction for all stakeholders. She could see that her old ways of viewing others and her role were contributing to disconnection and dissatisfaction. Recognizing that she had control of her own mindset, attitude, and behaviours, she set out to learn and upgrade all of them. She chose to shift her context (sensemaking) and her content (attitude and behaviour).

She began to talk less, interrupt less, and listen more to her internal clients and her manager. Her perspective was enriched and informed by their views. She saw opportunities to make adjustments to her own point of view. These were reflected in the kinds of statements she now made (fewer "should" statements) and greater solicitation of others' suggestions about what could be acceptable solutions.

She clearly could see her biases at work were, in fact, working against her best efforts to be an effective HR partner. Over time and with practice, she began to recognize where they would arise, and interrupted them before she spoke or took action. Her willingness to adjust in conversation, moving progressively towards mutually satisfactory solutions, was a testament to her intention and flexibility. She still could be informed by policies and procedures, yet think creatively about how to work well within them. She could work with both objective and subjective data, including them in her considerations for how best to move forward.

Many of the assumptions she previously held became the focus of a systematic review and overhaul. With perspective, she could identify many outdated assumptions worthy of dropping. There were others that were simply inappropriate for her work context and, once identified, could also be dropped. In general, she carefully reflected on the lenses she was wearing, how she was viewing the world, and the ways she had been making sense of it. In turn, her new, emergent mindset supported new kinds of conversations with a different emotional tone, and new behaviours to engage in, consistent with her HR role.

Her manager, in conversations with Donna, noticed the changes she was making, including her attitudinal shifts, tonal shifts, changes in logic, and decrease in defensiveness. Her clients as well began to see conversational and attitudinal changes in a positive direction. Infrequently, she would relapse into her reactive, defensive posture, often exacerbated by situational stress and her insufficiently developed effective stress response. She showed clear progress but not perfection.

At the end of the day, the CEO and COO were dissatisfied by how much progress Donna had made and were still ruminating over "prior bad acts". At their insistence, she was let go. Sometimes, this is what a successful outcome looks like for both organizational customers and coaching client stakeholders. The organization is able to make a staffing adjustment to better meet its needs; the coaching client can seek a better fit with another organization.

That is what happened with Donna. The company took the opportunity to reorganize its talent management/HR function to better fit its new shared services approach. Donna, with a strong recommendation from her manager, was soon hired by a different company in a different industry, has been thriving, and was recently promoted. She is doing excellent work, is positively challenged, and is very satisfied with her life and the opportunities ahead.

Key take-aways from this chapter

The larger game we are playing is how to be effective in our endeavours when our automatic approach fails to get the job done. We know we must be mindful to accomplish each of the subsequent steps well. We know that we need to be curious and wonder why we contributed to the breakdown we now want to resolve. And we recognize the perspective taking[19] (or perspective shifting) that will enable our new thinking and approaches towards success.

In pursuit of our goals, knowing our current reality is essential to making choices that move us in the right direction. If we do not know where we stand now – our current reality – we don't have a point of reference for moving towards our future. The next movement of the dance is to inquire further about how to keep going. As the 19th century French novelist Marcel Proust said, "The real voyage of discovery consists not in seeking new lands but seeing with new eyes."

CHAPTER 6

'I' is for Inquiry

Investigate, Integrate, and Inspire (3-I's)

Your leadership moment. The curtain rises and everyone looks to you. They count on you. A solution must be found. You take the helm. You're it.[1]

Here and now, this very minute, you stand at the crossroads of the past and the future. "Now" is where your thoughts and actions occur in real time. This may sound obvious, and still for many, only their bodies exist in the present while their thoughts and emotions are firmly and habitually focused on what could happen (future) or what has happened (past). Effective leaders recognize that in moments of crisis, giving undue regard to past experiences or what the future may hold reinforces uncertainty, and can undermine confidence about how to find a way forward.

The MYPRISM model emerged from working with leaders who recognize that as uncertainty rises, confidence fluctuates. Skilled leaders have adopted reliable methods to loosen the deep grip of habits and assumptions born of fear and uncertainty. They are self-aware and know how to recentre, become curious, and soften focus as information starts to pour in. By getting off autopilot and focusing on the moment, they avoid defaulting to habits, jumping too quickly to conclusions, or solving a problem before it is ripe for solution. MYPRISM is a leadership set of practices that anyone can integrate into their repertoire to enhance their capacity to lead capably at a moment's notice.

This chapter is about Inquiry, the "I" in MYPRISM. It is about the questions we ask and the relative degree of urgency behind finding one answer over another. This chapter introduces a repeatable methodology to secure timely and accurate information before making a decision.

The three processes of the Inquiry model (the "3-I's") are Investigate, Integrate, and Inspire.

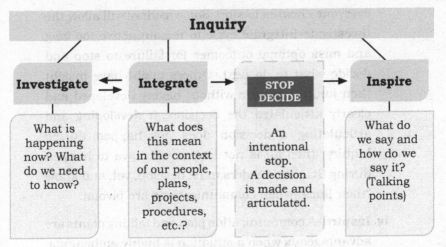

Figure 6.1. The 3 I's of Inquiry

i. **Investigate** – Something out of the ordinary captures your attention. You sense disruption. Choose trusted and capable others to assist with asking questions, triaging the threatening unknowns, and gathering relevant research, opinions, and facts from a broad cross-section of sources.

ii. **Integrate** – When a leader creates a culture that values and incentivises the gathering, curating, and sharing of information, the information flow will be robust and current, and the likelihood of disruptive surprises will be reduced. Regular meetings (or "integration sessions") dedicated to exploiting such information resources and making new findings could expose likely impacts upon the organization's goals, purpose, values, "brand", operations, and finances. Questions that emerge from an integration session are assigned, and the follow-up investigation commences.

iii. **Stop and Decide** – This point is not treated as an additional part of the Inquire model, because not everyone chooses to stop. Some leaders will allow the Investigate-Integrate cycle to remain active too long and miss optimal outcomes for failure to stop and decide what to do next. Others might have insight then jump to Inspire without having developed and clearly articulated the decision. If developing and articulating a decision does not happen during Inquiry, then all is not lost: it will have to happen during Staging. Leaders must develop, vet, and know "their lines" when communications are pivotal.

iv. Inspire –A communication plan and talking points are advantageous when a situation is highly ambiguous, complex, or explosive. People depend upon leaders when uncertainty is high and the MYPRISM process reminds leaders to communicate frequently, clearly, and directly. When addressing disruption, a prismatic leader would take time to consider what to say to rally others, and it is recommended that communications be delivered through multiple modes to increase the odds of being "heard" by the greatest number of people who are likely to have a variety of preferred learning styles.

Case Study #1

Amanda
Failure to Investigate

Amanda is a senior vice president of a national bank that made construction loans for mixed and affordable income residential developments. Amanda, situated in the home office, had worked for the bank for fifteen years when the COVID-19 pandemic led to company-wide consolidations, branch closures, and layoffs. She learned about the pending consolidation 30 days before it was scheduled to begin. At that time, she was too busy to learn more about the people who would report to her, the active projects, or the trouble-spots that would fall to her after the consolidation was implemented.

Victor was a recently promoted vice president at a branch office, but the consolidation plan led to his layoff. All of Victor's direct reports would be transitioned to Amanda because she had seniority and the competence to manage the teams virtually, with occasional on-site visits. Victor accepted a severance package.

Oliver, a senior director, was one of Victor's direct reports who transitioned to Amanda's team. Victor and Oliver had become more than work friends. They played golf every Sunday, their families socialized, and they travelled together. Oliver liked working with Victor, and felt protective of his friend, especially as Victor expressed anxiety about finding another job. Oliver had an idea. He decided that he would undermine Amanda's supervision and find ways to help her fail. Oliver knew that if something went wrong at the branch, Amanda would be blamed. Oliver figured that eventually Amanda's failures would be intolerable, and Victor would be brought back.

Oliver immediately resisted Amanda's authority and refused to respectfully engage with her. He withheld critical information, keeping Amanda out of the loop regarding several projects and personnel matters. Oliver made a point of disparaging Amanda's leadership and questioning her competence every day, with anyone who would listen – especially with his direct reports at team meetings.

As soon as she arrived to take over Victor's role, Amanda felt Oliver's resistance. She did not know much about him or what was bothering him, and she did not want to intrude by asking. So, Amanda chose to give Oliver more time and space to adjust, trusting that he knew how to do his job well. After several months, nothing had changed between them. Oliver's resentments festered with each passing week, and his negativity seeped into other relationships. Morale, productivity, and engagement plummeted. Customers started to complain about Oliver's unreliability.

Amanda received reports that Oliver unilaterally recommended approval of several high-risk loans, and defaults were looming. His direct reports and other employees across the company complained that Oliver was leaving documents unreviewed or unsigned and not answering emails or texts. Deals were not closing on time and borrowers were losing opportunities.

Amanda felt her blood run cold when she realized that she did not know where to begin to fix things. Four months had passed, and she and Oliver had yet to have a one-on-one meeting because he continued to cancel their appointments. Oliver simply refused to introduce Amanda to the projects, key customer contacts, regulators, and agents at other external funding sources.

Amanda scheduled a meeting with the president to discuss the situation. After disclosing her concerns, the president said that Oliver was too valuable to lose at this time, and that she should try harder to make it work. They agreed that HR would call Oliver to a meeting to see whether they could figure out what could be done to improve his communication and engagement with Amanda and others. Amanda left the meeting feeling unsupported, vulnerable, and anxious. She had no choice but to accept Oliver's protected status and create workarounds.

Oliver's meeting with HR went well. He was told he was valuable to the bank and was asked to try a little harder to communicate with Amanda. He left feeling secure and encouraged that his plan to sabotage Amanda seemed to be working.

As a last-ditch effort to assert her authority, Amanda decided to withhold Oliver's full bonus, hoping to send a message that insubordination has consequences. In response, Oliver quit, blamed Amanda, and refused to transition his projects and customer notes to her in a professional and timely manner.

Amanda had secretly hoped, but never planned, for Oliver's departure. Relief quickly turned to fear as she faced how much she did not know. Who in Oliver's network needed to be contacted immediately? Which projects were nearing deadlines? Who were the key external and internal stakeholders he depended upon or answered to? She worried about working with team members whose opinions of her might have been irretrievably tarnished by Oliver's gossip. Amanda felt painfully ashamed of herself for not having successfully confronted Oliver about his behaviour. She was to blame, she thought. She failed to manage Oliver well. Amanda could not sleep at night. How was she supposed to lead her department confidently into the future when she was overwhelmed by all the to-dos and should-haves? She had let herself down and failed the president who had made it clear that Oliver was valuable, and she had to make the situation work. Maybe she was just not good enough to do the job. Should she resign before making another mistake?

Uncertainty Is Uncomfortable!

Amanda's reality was fraught. In the grip of self-doubt, self-loathing, and self-destructive mental habits, she lost her ability to view and assess reality with objectivity and curiosity. Could MYPRISM have helped Amanda regain composure and control? The answer: *Yes, in one of two ways*.

If Amanda were new to MYPRISM, she could have proceeded stepwise through the MYPRISM process, greatly enhancing calmness and clarity. Or, if Amanda already had incorporated MYPRISM into her leadership practices, she might have entirely avoided the breakdown with Oliver. Confident and calm leaders keep the MYPRISM practice "always on" in the background. Had Amanda already integrated MYPRISM into her leadership practice she would have walked into her new circumstances with more information, perspective, and the buoyancy needed to bounce back and forward in the face of novel or acutely challenging circumstances.

Investigate

What do we need to know?

As the stakes rise, active curiosity has a steady, direct, and regenerative impact on the thoughts we have, and on the choices we make.[2] An intentional shift of mindset from "fix-it!" to "what's missing?" quells anxiety and reactivates one's innate desire to learn. Amanda did zero investigation when she learned about the planned consolidation. Under pressure from the upcoming change, on top of the responsibilities she already had, Amanda did not have the leadership know-how to pause, assess the possible threats, and identify and enlist others who might help her prepare for the change. Amanda's business-as-usual, autopilot approach prevented her from imagining what might be different, so she detrimentally assumed that she knew all she needed to know to get started, thinking she could deal with everything after moving into the new position. How Amanda would show up at a time of crisis would set the tone for those looking to her for leadership. Unfortunately, Amanda showed up oblivious to the level of disgruntlement that she would find when she stepped into Victor's shoes.

In a crisis, a leader's objective is to identify ways forward that promise to advance the organization's goals while doing the least amount of harm. Optimal investigation involves energizing others with similar concerns to set out physically, emotionally, and intellectually to discover and test what options are available and viable. Collaborative investigation involves six steps.

Six Steps of Investigation

1. **Get Grounded** – Notice that emotions have been activated (shallow breathing, rapid heart rate, anxiety, jumbled thoughts). Breathe deeply a few times with a longer exhale than inhale. Acknowledge that something significant is happening, that

you will play a key part, and that you can handle whatever comes your way. Notice and label your emotions because emotions are data and recognizing them can provide opportunities for self-correction and situational awareness. Emotions are contagious so it helps to be clear about whose emotions you are feeling; are they yours or are you being overly empathetic and feeling someone else's?

2. **Get Clear** – Focus on the present to assess your role and responsibilities. Consider what outcomes would be ideal or acceptable. Develop initial hypotheses of what else might be possible. Put the current reality in perspective and develop a clear statement for stakeholders about the situation.

3. **Assemble an A-Team of the Trusted** – Look inside and outside the organization to identify allies and experts who could be affected or share your concerns. Choose people loyal to and protective of you, as well as naysayers and disruptors. Meet to explore the facts and circumstances from many angles. Generate questions that must be addressed, air ideas that could be relevant, and prioritize what must be figured out first, second, and third to advance a robust understanding of the situation.

4. **Assign Roles and Responsibilities** – Bearing in mind the diversity of skills, experiences, personalities, and vulnerabilities among individuals, determine roles and responsibilities. Who will research what? What decision-making authority does each have and with what must they return to the group before acting? As leader, determine what *only you* can do and reserve that domain for yourself.

5. **Set expectations** – Communicate how you want the findings of your team presented and set a deadline. Decide whether and when you want individuals to check in with you prior to the deadline. Make clear the consequences of a significant failure to generate accurate and pertinent information. Make clear the advantages of and opportunities that could flow from successful research.

6. **Release** – Release individuals to their quest to collect and preliminarily analyze their data, keeping yourself available for consultation upon request. Keep your attention on the evolving situation and how that evolution may affect an optimal outcome.

Case Study #2

James
Failure to Integrate

James owns a small non-profit made up of consultants and caregivers who design and manage plans for disabled persons' long-term physical or intellectual special needs. In this vulnerable population, emergencies occur every day, including medical emergencies, discrimination, bullying, or looming financial ruin. These events cause clients acute distress, and many calls require immediate attention.

Before the COVID-19 pandemic, the office was bustling and buzzing with mission-driven collaboration. Every employee answered the office phones and could walk down the hall to enlist the assistance of a team member. James' expertise, involvement, and dedication to client service ensured that procedures were followed, and every client was provided consistent, expert, caring support.

When the first state-wide COVID-19 stay-at-home orders were announced, James investigated the situation and quickly concluded that, indeed, there was a contagious and deadly virus on the loose, but that the work from home ("WFH") orders were largely panic-driven and overblown. Furthermore, James considered how WFH would affect the non-profit's clients, its "brand", and its revenue. It seemed obvious to James at the time that he was in the perfect position to figure out what was best for everybody. He had to act fast and did not ask for others' input.

The decision was announced: *"Due to the vulnerable nature of our clients, no one will be permitted to work from home. All employees are to show up, practice social distancing at work, and use caution when they are not in the office."* James emphasized that everyone had a private office with a door, so personnel could isolate in their offices and only walk down the hall when warranted. This approach would keep the flow of information, collaboration, and responsive customer service in full effect, while allowing for moderate sequestration.

This "top-down" order was met with disappointment and resentment, which festered. When two employees contracted COVID-19, anxiety surged, and James' credibility and perceived trustworthiness plummeted. Several employees called in sick the following week, then the office manager, an employee with diabetes, and a new intern quit. Those who came to work did not emerge from their offices until the end of the day.

What went wrong? Why did employees who shared James's passion for the work, and who cared deeply for clients, not get on board with his decision? James believed he had demonstrated countless times in the past that decisions were made with everyone's best interests in mind. Blinded by assumptions, biases, and fears, James' ability to think critically was compromised. He failed to consider individual differences and other intangible adverse forces at work. He failed to acknowledge that the pandemic had dismantled shared beliefs about safety in the office, causing familiar employees to react to the new health threats in unpredictable ways.

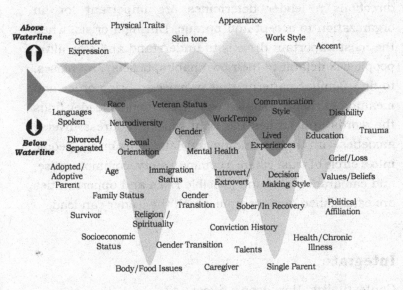

Figure 6.2. The Iceberg
Copyright © Jennifer Brown Consulting, 2022; All Rights Reserved

Valued employees had their own trusted social networks and news sources. Instead of understanding employees' circumstances, and mitigating their varied fears through open communication, James triggered resistance and revolt. He failed to anticipate how authoritative leadership under unprecedented conditions could undermine the goodwill he had established. When James chose not to include others in consideration of how to face the crisis, employees lost trust that James was putting their needs on par with his own.

The dynamic of human unpredictability is depicted by Jennifer Brown, in *How to be an Inclusive Leader*.[3] The graphic "The Iceberg," shown in Figure 6.2 shows what may lie beneath the surface of a person's presence. Everyone has a personal history and things about themselves that they prefer to keep hidden. These below-surface factors are the forces at work for or against the decisions and directions a leader determines are important for an organization to accept and pursue. During a crisis, when the most important drive is to understand and stay alive, people will default to their own habits, beliefs, and biases, to find familiar patterns that promise to bring order and meaning to their disrupted world. The skilled leader finds the words and strikes the right tone to address diverse anxieties with understanding and calm. This brings people into a circle of trust where a common story, common cause, and camaraderie around possible risks and opportunities are established, a place from which the leader can lead.

Integrate

Contextualize. How does it affect us?

To integrate is to incorporate into; to unite with something else.[4] A collaborative team committed to dogged, iterative fact-finding will uncover rich and broad sources of current information. When they reassemble to discuss findings, contextualization helps them put the data and theories into a meaningful reality making it possible to estimate whether and how much something could help or hinder progress, help or hurt certain individuals, or impact the larger organization. When new questions arise mid-course, new roles and responsibilities are assigned, and the team goes out again to retrieve pertinent information.

Investigate–integrate could go on indefinitely unless the leader knows when it is time to stop and decide.

To keep a team "of one mind" and the rudder true, below are a few questions leaders might ask or privately consider when integrating new information. These questions are designed to facilitate a reflective pause. The power of the MYPRISM practice is that the leader has a way to mitigate or pre-empt catastrophe by cultivating awareness of trends and occurrences.

- What strategic objective(s) are we pursuing?
- What new information has been discovered?
- How might the new information impact our objective(s)?
- What are the current best practices for managing similar disruptions?
- If the worst were to happen, what would that look like?
- What is within our control? What can we not control?
- What is an optimal outcome given what we now know?
- What opportunities – current or potential - are emerging?
- Whether and how does the new information align with our values (as individuals, as a group, as a community, as an institution)?
- Who are our allies among those who would be impacted? What information, insights, or support might they provide or need?
- What internal or external forces could get in the way? (Human, economic, cultural, time, etc.)
- How might a decision based on the relevant new

information affect the bottom line? The organization's competitiveness?

- What do we still need to know? How will we find out? Who will do what next?

Investigate-Integrate provides a powerful way to stay current while all team members actively participate in discovery, dialogue, and evaluation of possible threats and opportunities. Day to day, this practice leverages people's natural curiosity and need to belong to a community. Calling for regular, brief, focused huddles (meetings) to report out findings provides valuable time and space for team members to communicate consistently with one another, and hold one another accountable. Skilled leaders know whether to run the huddles weekly, monthly, or daily; it will depend upon the novelty and urgency of issues that arise, and on the rhythm of the industry you are in (fast-paced such as news organizations; slow-paced such as large-scale engineering).

Investigation and inquiry, valuable processes that they are, could go on too long and have negative consequences. When meetings shift from routine information sharing to reactive and pivotal "problem solving", difficult decision making will follow. The Investigation and Inquiry must cease to allow skilled leaders to pause and make decisions when the pressure is on or when uncertainty still prevails. How is someone to know when enough is enough?

Optimal Stopping

When Investigate, Integrate, Inspire ("I-I-I")
becomes "Aye Yay Yay"

Warning: Well-intentioned and purposeful collaboration may lead to analysis paralysis and gratuitous inclusivity.

Imagine facilitating an energized, collaborative, and coordinated process where able and trusted colleagues are actively out investigating what an organization needs to know and then returning for robust collaborative analysis of the new data and its implications. What could be better than being part of an engaging, intellectually stimulating, and productive workplace? If questions beget more questions wrapped in further uncertainty, what can a responsible leader leave unstudied, undiscovered, undone? How does a leader know when to stop the cycle, call the question, make a decision, and start staging for execution? A combination of intuition, wisdom, rational analysis, and experience helps.

The authors of *Algorithms to Live By*[5] propose a data-based way of knowing when to stop and decide amid uncertainty, rapid change, time constraints, and imperfect information. If you make the decision too soon, you might miss the best option, but if you wait too long, you might waste valuable time and resources by holding out for the optimal solution that does not exist. The authors present an algorithm that calculates the balance point between investigation and optimal stopping to make a decision.

Their algorithm posits that optimal stopping comes at 37% of the amount of time or options available. The "Look-Then-Leap Rule" proposes the following methodology. The decision maker sets a predetermined amount of time for "looking" – exploring options, gathering data, and reviewing. The decision makers refrain from choosing any one option no matter how efficacious an option might seem. Then, after 37% of the time has passed, or 37% of available options have been reviewed, you "leap," that is, commit to the option that equals or outshines the best idea you have come across in the "look" phase.

While it may be false precision to suggest that all decisions are best made in some specific fraction of the time one might expect to be needed, the results of the studies reported in *Algorithms to Live By* show how important it is to develop a sense for when enough Investigate-Integrate is enough. Whether Optimal Stopping is considered an algorithmic formula or a leadership skill, knowing how and when to stop is needed for a variety of applications. Once the well-informed decision is made, then it is time to communicate "what, why, how, and when" in a manner designed to Inspire others to join.

Inspire

Communications Plan

Are you wondering why Inspire is part of Inquiry? It is because the higher the stakes, the more heightened the emotions, or the bigger the audience, the more essential it becomes that your communications hit the mark and inspire. Even the most charismatic leaders prepare if they hope to evoke inspiration.

Leading a company, a team, a family, a country, or a cause all require leadership skills, just of varying degrees and consequences. In that capacity, it helps to pause, check what you're going to say, who you will be saying it to, and how you're going to say it. And how do you want others to experience your leadership when you deliver a message? What specifically do you want them to remember most from everything you will say? Some people hire speechwriters because it is very difficult to inspire, to get the words, state of mind and heart, and delivery just right.

Fear and Curiosity are Good for Inspiration

"The oldest and strongest emotion of mankind is fear, and the oldest and strongest kind of fear is fear of the unknown". H.P. Lovecraft

Human beings are born to struggle and survive. Inspiration is most needed and welcomed when people feel frightened, neglected, or confused. What distinguishes one leader from another is how well each can tolerate uncertainty. People with a high tolerance for uncertainty stay curious longer and hold off self-soothing decision-making until data and intuition reveal the best next step.

Skilled leaders see disruption and the fear that follows as an opportunity to help people through the fog, because people depend more upon others and their communities when uncertainty and possible danger rise up. A leader's inspiring comments help people see new possibilities, especially when delivered in ways and words that convey, *your concerns have been heard and understood.*

A leader who remains composed and purposeful in the face of disruption and fear can de-escalate collective tension. Uncertainties become puzzles, fear yields to curiosity, and vulnerability grows into collective purpose.

When crafting a message to inspire, pausing to gain clarity about a target audience's beliefs, needs, and fears is a best practice for crafting a call to action that evokes the feelings and insights the leader endorses. When fear[6] is present, then the skilled leader will acknowledge and speak to that fear during communications in ways that ease tension and provide space for the emotions to transform into more constructive thoughts and feelings.

> *"Nothing in life is to be feared. It is only to be understood. Now is the time to understand more, so that we may fear less." Marie Curie (1867-1934)*

Leaders who can alleviate the grip of reactive emotions and inspire curiosity instead will drive performance[7], engagement, courage, and enjoyment[7] at work. Curiosity is a wakeup call that something important, relevant, or fascinating remains unknown. Many researchers agree[8] that curiosity is the best predictor of strength in critical leadership competencies such as good decision making. Leaders who inspire others to see themselves not as victims but as active participants in finding opportunities and solutions will create loyal and productive allies at every level of an organization. It is always worth spending time to craft communications before jumping into action.

Conclusion

3-I Leadership: A Way of Being

While writing this chapter, we had an opportunity to discuss the MYPRISM model with a trusted colleague who is the CEO of a national organization with more than 8000 employees. She listened carefully as we spoke. When we finished, she said, "Wow, that's a lot to remember!" Their comments underscore an important, if not obvious, point that it is not helpful to apply any leadership or problem-solving model when you need it most if it is a struggle to remember it. Leadership requires mental, emotional, and physical discipline, along with regular practice. Skilled leaders develop the art of *Inquiry* as outlined in this chapter, along with other skills, by practicing until the skills operate subconsciously and are always accessible. Prismatic leaders appear calm in a crisis because they do not have to change what they do; they merely need to turn up the intensity and pace of the Investigate, Integrate, <stop>, Inspire triad. Being aware in the present and inquiring collaboratively about the impact of new information empowers leaders to step forward with compassion, curiosity, and power when the people they lead need them most.

CHAPTER 7

"S" is for Staging

Mike had been charged with aligning a recently merged company's IT systems with the parent company's infrastructure. The decision had been made; it was time to implement the decision. Mike walked into the meeting where he and his counterparts from the merged organization were set to work out the details, and proceeded to push, cajole, and lay it "all down" so that everyone would get moving. There was no time or money to waste. Two days later, he was in front of his boss and HR discussing a complaint that had arisen from that meeting – a complaint charging him with being uncollaborative, bullying, and myopic in his approach. As a result, his leadership capability was being questioned: Did he really have what it takes to shepherd such a critical project to a successful end?

The temptation to move to action can be fierce; we tend to rush headlong to operationalize our decisions. At the opposite end is the lure of analysis paralysis: keeping still while sinking into endless permutations of *how* to act.

At another company, Yeni worked in the highly regulated, high-pressure, high-speed world of pharmaceutical production. Data drove the industry but so did a focus on quality and speed to market. Although Yeni was talented and had a capable team that could easily manage the work volume, production was behind schedule and there seemed to be more open projects than finished products. In stepping back and looking at how she worked, Yeni realized that at almost every stage of the process, she dove in deep to think about all the possible ways her team could tackle issues; she also reached out and "checked in" with all key stakeholders, and re-created reports and presentations to fit her stakeholders' communication styles. Each of these actions, by themselves, were laudable. However, in aggregate, they were forcing Yeni and her team to move at a glacial pace that could not support the organization's production goals. Yeni, in doing all the "right things", was failing.

Can there be a balance between doing the right thing while still moving forward at a reasonable and productive pace?

This is where *staging* comes in.

Staging is the process of actively designing how we engage, execute, and exit once a decision has been made. It is about proactively orchestrating the movements, resources, and speed by which we reach our goals. At its very core, staging is about planning and orchestrating a masterful implementation.

Part of the magic in theatre is experiencing a cacophony of elements seamlessly coming together to create the impact called for in the moment. The set, the actors, the lighting, the clothes – every element on stage has a purpose. This is staging come to life through the purposeful preparation for and visualisation of the final outcome.

Staging Engagement

Mike's rush to action was by no means unusual. As leaders, we are trained and rewarded to solve problems and measure success, without appreciating that many business problems cannot be solved without taking the time to manage the relationships involved. The accompanying emotions and behaviours linked to these relationships are not bugs, but rather relevant data that can inform our approach to and engagement with the challenges we face.

As leaders, we can practice the art of staging as we carry out our intentions and decisions. Reflecting on the following questions will help us deliberately and mindfully engage with the project with the end in mind[1]:

What is the gist?

A gist is essentially a short summary, usually 100-200 words, of the most important points, the most relevant data, and the key factors that describe the environment we are working with. Eliminating all extraneous information allows us to have a clear focus not only on the results we are looking for, but also on the key considerations and actions we will need to successfully produce those results. Skipping this question caused Mike to succumb to tunnel vision, seeing only what he thought was important versus what was actually needed.

How do I want to be described at the end of this situation?

Mike understood how critical the project was for his career and the organization. He knew the "why" behind the project and what success could and should look like. After the talk with HR, Mike knew he had to change his approach in order to successfully implement the project. "How do I want to be described at the end of this situation?" helped Mike think about how he could show up as his "best self", even in the most stressful of circumstances. As he became more comfortable staging engagement, he added other questions to his reflections: What would be the sense of gravitas he brought to critical negotiations? What level of warmth balanced with logical rigor did he want and need to apply? What kind of leader did he want to be, not only to his team, but to his new colleagues? Visualizing how he wanted to show up in the critical moments of the project and with the difficult personalities he had to navigate helped him anchor and direct his energy to create the needed impact, regardless of the challenges he faced.

What will others care about? What will they need?

Designing how we engage means not only thinking about how we show up but also thinking about how others want to be perceived, and how they want their concerns addressed – without ignoring our own priorities. This is why staging is so critical for a leader's success. As you design your engagement with others, you can diagnose the likely challenges and the compromises you will be able to make without endangering your goals.

Yeni's original approach was to abandon her needs for the sake of others. This approach did not reflect leadership, but rather abdication. To correct this, Yeni shifted gears and began "contracting" with her stakeholders by clarifying not only goals and roles but also mutual accountabilities and how she would work with others. In these "contracting" conversations they explored these key questions:

- What needs to be achieved?
- Who needs to do what to achieve the desired outcomes?
- What should be the cadence of interactions – specifically, the timing and rhythm of key interactions?
- How would they escalate issues?
- What were some non-negotiables?

Once Yeni worked with others so there was a mutual understanding of accountabilities, the bottleneck eased.

What resources do we have, what will we need?

Staging engagement is about visualizing the first moment of action and playing out what materials, resources, information, and people will be required to create the desired outcome. However, this is not simply a checklist. There needs to be a deeper understanding and clarity around the following key questions:

- Who needs what resources and when?

- Who is the best provider of these resources? What is Plan B if these are not available?

- Does the team have strong interpersonal relationships to weather the challenges ahead? If not, how can these relationships be strengthened?

- What is the organizational/industry climate in which the team will need to operate? Will they need additional support?

- Is everyone's understanding aligned around these questions and their answers?

What will I need access to?

In designing how we engage, we cannot forget the basic resources needed to execute on our decision – not only the materials and the data, but more importantly, access to critical stakeholders. One of the reasons contracting worked well for Yeni's shift was that she was able to outline who had access and who would facilitate access to critical stakeholders to keep production moving. She no longer operated under the assumption that access would simply be available; she staged and contracted for it, easing the execution process.

We might be tempted, after successfully designing how we engage at the beginning of the project or initiative, to gloss over what needs to happen as we execute. After all, if we had a good start, everything should run smoothly, right? In truth, to paraphrase Helmuth von Moltke, a German Field Marshal of the 19th century: *"no plan survives first contact with the enemy."*

Staging Execution

One of the reasons there was such pressure on Mike to integrate the new organization's systems into the parent company was that this integration had, surprisingly, stalled badly. However, in the rush to "get it done," Mike forgot the overarching purpose behind his mandate. Yes, the company needed to save money and yes, it needed to become more efficient. However, the integration process needed to support the merger of two cultures, of two distinct ways of working. In this process, he had an opportunity to *model* how to problem solve, how to innovate, and how to work together with the new teams. Such was the ultimate "why" of his mandate. In designing the execution of the integration, re-visiting the "why" of the work helped Mike stay focused during countless meetings and negotiations. When he felt the need to bulldoze opposition, he reminded himself that the goal of this effort was to create a new culture and a new work paradigm, which allowed him to step back and try an approach that would both move the work forward and build towards this overarching goal.

Mindfulness is thus critical when staging execution. When the pressure is on and our anxieties around failure emerge, we can ensnare ourselves in survival mode rather than leading with strength of purpose. How and when do we build moments of collective reflection with our teams that keep us mindful of our movements and impact? The answer lies in intentionally designing touch points to reflect on how we are working together and whether the original plan is still working. These touch points give everyone on the team the space to diagnose problems and proactively deal with them. However, diagnosing and proactively dealing with problems only happen if we, as leaders, underscore the importance of these mindful reflection moments and are willing to follow through on what we learned from them. By invoking the curious and inquiring mind, Yeni and Mike revisited how to actively involve the team members in collective inquiry - investigation, integration, and inspiration - during the critical Staging phase for execution.

To successfully stage execution, reflect on these questions:

How do I design follow through?

Leaders go into action with the full intention to get to the finish line, yet lack of follow-through is one of the most common complaints from teams about their leaders. After a strong plan has been created, we can get distracted, lose focus and energy, leaving our teams feeling rudderless and, sometimes, abandoned. Why does that happen?

Does it have to be a sprint or a marathon?

How many times have you found yourself and others just saying, "I'm tired" or "I don't have time to think?" In designing execution, we often overlook how we will manage our energy levels, or how we will manage our team's energy levels. Jane Fonda recently spoke about her work around activism. She reflected that in her early years, she thought of her work as a sprint; later in life, as she matured, she saw it as a marathon. Today, she views her activist work as a relay race meant to spread out the work so you can amplify your impact through others.[2]

Why not think of our work as leaders in those terms? There are moments when, as leaders, we will need to carry all the burden on our shoulders. We alone will need to make the sprint. However, that does not have to be every single second. We can identify those "burden" moments and plan on how we will build our energy to make those moments a success. We can carve out the time we will need to recover. We can also clearly identify when the work should be more of a relay race and have conversations with others on what we will need to do to ensure everyone maintains their batteries fully charged to get to the end. When we fail to follow through because our energy is depleted, we surrender to a vortex of activity and forget to lead. Re-energizing ourselves and our teams is a decision point we can design into our execution plan; it is only accessible through our self-awareness. It is our choice to make it happen.

Upon reflection, Mike now believes that his depleted energy was a major contributing factor that led to the disastrous HR meeting. Feeling depleted made it hard for him to gain perspective and understand what had actually occurred. When Mike was sitting in front of his boss and HR, he kept asking himself, "What is wrong with the people on my team?" For a long time, he felt that they were entitled and that they did not "get it". Rather than consider that he had mis-stepped, he attributed their feedback to a flaw in their characters. Yet, there was nothing wrong with his new colleagues. They simply wanted what everyone wants when working with others, especially in challenging times: psychological safety.[3]

How can I stage for psychological safety during execution?

As leaders, we may try to be empathetic, to address everyone's concerns, and to create safety – all while keeping our hands firmly on the steering wheel. However, when designing execution, our key stakeholders and team members might be better served if we pause and ask them what they need. In opening the door for discussion with the larger group, they can co-create with us the guardrails they need and are willing to follow, thus creating safety for everyone on the team. As leaders we do not have a magic wand; instead, we have the opportunity to create a safe environment for the team by allowing them to offer their input and buy-in into how to address the challenge. Creating this safe environment can start with a simple question: "What would help you...?". When Mike asked this question of the team, it allowed him to reset and re-engage with them on a stronger footing.

Psychological safety is particularly critical in using our "ability to rethink and unlearn"[4]. As Adam Grant describes in Think Again[5]:

> *"Some psychologists point out that we're mental misers: we often prefer the ease of hanging on to old views over the difficulty of grappling with new ones. Yet there are also deeper forces behind our resistance to rethinking. Questioning ourselves makes the world more unpredictable. It requires us to admit that the facts may have changed, that what was once right may now be wrong. Reconsidering something we believe deeply can threaten our identities, making it feel as if we're losing a part of ourselves."*

Our ability to pivot during a challenge, to be comfortable with the unpredictable, could make the ultimate difference in the level of our success. Compassion for ourselves and the psychological safety for others makes it a little easier to turn off our autopilot and make that intentional pivot towards a better path forward, bringing others along with us.

What are the stories I will need to share? What are the stories I will need to hear?

Yeni was fantastic at creating psychological safety, primarily by ensuring that she communicated, or rather, overcommunicated with others. Ensuring that everyone has the information they need to move forward, at the right time, is a fundamental aspect of staging execution. However, one of the reasons Yeni felt she had to re-create presentations and continuously check in with stakeholders was that it seemed that the information she needed her stakeholders to pay attention to never seemed to land, much less "stick". She thus set about making communications more effective by planning how to cascade critical information so that it was "sticky"[6]. Yeni started to design into her execution "storytelling" – clearly synthesizing (not summarizing) critical information[7] so she and other key stakeholders could evangelize and activate this information as needed.

As we design execution, we can identify the moments when we may need to engage in storytelling to gain support, to motivate, and to propel forward movement. We can also start cataloguing the key points and stories that will allow us to, as McKinsey's Charles Conn writes in Six problem-solving mindsets for very uncertain times, "present the argument emotionally as well as logically and show why the preferred action offers an attractive balance between risks and rewards".[8]

There is an unexpected benefit to storytelling: in helping our audience to capture and retain key data, it also invites discourse. As Yeni prioritized what to share via storytelling, she not only engaged her stakeholders but also opened the door to cognitive diversity[9]. She listened to her stakeholders' stories, allowing for multiple perspectives to come through and help her be better informed in the moment, thus accelerating her decisions and execution.

What is enough?

In staging execution, we can become paralyzed – the very thing we are trying to avoid through staging – if we overthink all the possible details, interactions, challenges, and opportunities. Yeni's thinking and work style made her susceptible to this trap. She always joked that her spreadsheets had spreadsheets, and each cell had a formula. What helped her break this habit was the combination of self-awareness and mindfulness anchored by the question "What is enough?" Sometimes, leaders need to build the plane while they fly it. This question allowed Yeni to prioritize those moments based on the needs of the team and the project, not her comfort.

Still, it might be difficult to know when enough is enough. This is where feedback and strong, honest relationships with our key stakeholders is critical. Asking, debating, and exploring what is needed for optimal results, what will be the differentiating factor that creates success, and what is extraneous and a waste of time can help us more realistically stage execution.

Staging The Exit

In thinking about how to mould all the different players in the project into a high-performing team[10], Mike realized he had never thought about the team's collective learning as a key ingredient for cohesiveness. For him, every person was responsible for their own growth during the project, before moving on, once the team was done with its assignment, to the other 100 things waiting for them. As part of the process, Mike did post-mortems, but upon reflection realized that those post-mortems were just checklists. Yes, the team learned what not to do the next time, but team members missed the opportunity to integrate those learnings into their day-to-day work. More importantly, they rushed through the project work so fast that they were not able to capitalize on the bonding opportunity the project presented. Mike decided he would create a new habit for the team – the habit to intentionally reflect, integrate, and bond. Creating this habit only took a few tweaks. Specifically, in the post-mortems he added two questions to discuss:

What did we learn?

Each person had to share something he or she had learned from or appreciated about another team member's contribution. This step highlighted the strengths available for everyone in the team to tap into; it ensured that team members had an opportunity to learn from their peers. It also built pride and trust in the team as a whole. Once team members had contributed their individual learnings, they wrapped up the discussion by exploring their *collective* learnings and how they wanted to integrate these into their day-to-day.

Where else do we see this?

This question allowed the members of the team to analyse where else in their work they were seeing similar patterns of behaviours, challenges, or strengths. It expanded their mindfulness beyond the immediate work they were reviewing to capture the patterns that helped or hindered them as a whole. Rather than Mike being the only one to look out for entrenched habits, for example, there was now a collective and powerful scan in place that helped to accelerate the team's learnings and bonding.

As we stage the exit, designing how we will synthesize our learnings is a small investment that typically yields great returns. In addition, when staging a pause to learn, we also have the opportunity to stage a moment to celebrate. On the theatre stage, actors receive thunderous applause for their extraordinary performance; how will we, as leaders, celebrate our team's achievements?

Lastly, beyond designing the exit, we can make a commitment to reflect if our original vision of success measures up to the reality – specifically, by calibrating the following questions with our experience:

- Does this fulfil our original goals? If so, how?
- Will I, as a leader, be able to look myself in the mirror and honestly say we have lived by our values? How will we hold ourselves accountable?

Staging is a practice that enables leaders to move confidently and at the right speed towards a masterful implementation. It is about creating an overall balanced and thoughtful orchestration of your and your team's talents, movements. and resources. Why not make the investment for such a powerful outcome?

What will you stage for success?

Key take-aways from this chapter

Staging Engagement	Staging Execution	Staging the Exit
What is the gist? How do I want to be described at the end of this situation?	How do I design follow-through?	What did we learn? Where else do we see this?
What will others care about? What will they need?	How can I stage for psychological safety during execution?	Does this fulfil our original goals? If so, how?
	What are stories I will need to share? What are the stories I will need to hear?	Will I, as a leader, be able to look myself in the mirror and honestly say we have lived by our values? How will we hold ourselves accountable?
	What is enough?	

CHAPTER 8

"M" is for Move

"Here we go again...", COO Dorothy whispered to CFO Fran. This was the fourth "ideation" meeting in the same number of weeks on the same topic of a "go-to-market operating model". The senior leadership team, comprising six of the most senior leaders in the company, had been discussing and reviewing various options presented by the Chief Strategy Officer. No decision was imminent. Everyone expected to be told to return to the drawing board for more research. After a four-hour session, the meeting was adjourned with a "well done, good job" from the CEO. But still no decision. This time, there was not even a "next step".

This scenario has been played out in many meetings across many organizations. It is the proverbial analysis paralysis. It also demonstrates a simple and obvious but often overlooked element in effective leadership: taking action. The last "M" in MYPRISM is for "Move". Without "move", all you will be left with are thoughts and maybe at best some insights. But insights alone do not lead to change. You will be hoping for a different result with the same, familiar actions of the past – what Einstein famously described as insanity.

Change is Hard

We are naturally wired to resist change. After all, the actions that brought us safely to the present seem to work: We survived, so why change? Such is our default *modus operandi*. This explains why we fear what we don't know – a fear that can drive us to stereotyping, prejudice, and even racism. We feel safest when there is certainty, familiarity, and routine. Unless there is tension or a "burning platform", we do not automatically opt to learn a new way. Hence, the saying "sink or swim": When thrown into the deep end, we will instantly take action to stay afloat. Otherwise, it is easier to rely on floating devices and just float along.

It does not always have to be this way. If we only change when there is a burning platform, we unnecessarily limit our creativity and leadership range. Over time, our cognitive muscle deteriorates. In moments of stress, we are left to rely on under-developed cognitive skills. In these situations, we resist change because our anxious brain is in high gear and our learning/creative brain is dormant. If we were to take a moment to address and soothe the anxious brain, the learning and creativity sides of our cognitive skills would have a better chance to demonstrate their extensive prowess. What else is possible? What else is better? We would find a way out, a way to survive and thrive. The challenge is not to be seized by our anxious brain. Courage is the ability to act despite fear.

Anxiety and lack of courage are just some of the reasons behind our inertia. The senior leadership team at the beginning of this chapter eventually realized they had to unpack the underlying reasons for their inability to make decisions and take action. After a few group coaching sessions, they understood and accepted that their collective fear of failure and the comfort of success were the barriers to action. "Let's *think* about change" was all they could manage. There was no tension to fuel any need to change. Their autopilot was to repeat the same go-to-market model selling the same products with the same features. Although the market was evolving and consumer behaviours were changing, they congratulated themselves on maintaining the status quo. They did not know any other way since they had not developed their ability to think creatively; and time only increased their resistance to transformation (or action). Each year, their financial performance was determined solely by consumer behaviour – or even the weather since the weather impacted consumer behaviour – over which they exerted no control. This autopilot model of repeating the past was definitely not immune to failure, especially in a VUCA world.

Breaking the inertia and making the first move

Think back to the "sink or swim" saying. What is the impetus for a non-swimmer to suddenly spring to action in the pool? Survival. The tension creates the need to learn. But tension need not always be borne of fear or threat. Indeed, recognizing this tension (e.g., fear of failure) is the first step towards positive and creative action. If you start training for a marathon by trying to run ten miles at the first try, you are unlikely to want to complete your training program. You are more likely to tell yourself, "This is too hard for me. I am not going to make it". You just reinforced your anxious brain. Unless you find another source of motivation, your anxious brain will soon be telling you to give up.

Conversely, imagine that in your first practice, you simply run as far and as fast or slow as your body will let you, with no judgment. At the end of the first run, you are more likely to feel good about your run. "I did it!" Congratulations! You are on your way to completing the marathon. Allow yourself to feel the joy of success. The anxious brain is soothed and begins to step back. It is now possible to visualize crossing the finishing line.

Ever wonder why most weight loss programs are not successful? Because most people give up. It is too difficult. However, if they start the program by first experiencing the joy of not gaining weight, their brain is more assured that weight loss is possible. Letting yourself experience the joy of success is the Theory of Self-Efficacy[1] in play. The theory, put simply, is this: If you believe you can, you are more likely to perform at that level. Simply believing you can, however, is not enough: you need to experience a successful performance. Having a vicarious experience through role models is one way to experience the required performance. "If others can do it, I can too." However, the best way to experience a successful performance is to do it yourself.

Business and management consultants often talk about "quick wins". The concept of quick wins is another manifestation of the Self-Efficacy Theory. Because it allows you to experience success, a quick win builds momentum and fuels motivation for the next bigger move. Quick wins energize the creative brain. To achieve a quick win, start small. Steady baby steps are important to the final sprint in the last half mile of the marathon.

In Chapter 2, we talked about the importance of being mindful – being acutely aware of your internal as well external conditions. In making your move, it is important to maintain that mindfulness. What is going on inside (your fears, anxiety, triggers, emotions) and outside (your environment, people you impact, people impacting you)? In your effort to be mindful, it is important to acknowledge what you can control vs. what you can influence vs. what you can only register as a concern but cannot do anything about (for now)[2].

We often overestimate what we control. For example, we like to think we control our environment. In truth, we really only control ourselves. Stephen Covey[3] provided a helpful list on what we can truly control:

- Our thoughts
- Our words
- Our action
- Our decisions
- Our attitude
- Our mood
- Our ethics

Note the emphasis on what we *can* control. This is deliberate. Just because we *can* does not automatically translate to, we *do*. Without mindfulness, our brain lulls us into thinking we are in control, but often we default to autopilot grounded by past experiences (including past traumas). The good news is that mindfulness is a practice. The more we practice, the better we are at achieving a high level of self-regulation in controlling what we can control. Tailor your actions on what you can control for maximum impact towards your "WHY" – your purpose (see the chapter on Y). Remember, you want more purposeful responses (actions) and less emotional reactions. Beyond "control", be mindfully alert on what you can "influence". Again, Stephen Covey provides good guidance on this subject. You can only hope to influence the items on the list that belong to others (e.g., their thoughts, their words, etc.). You influence through what you can control. Through your own conduct you start to influence others. As you increase your ability to control what you can control, your sphere of influence expands. The innovative, customer-focused front desk greeter can influence the company's approach to customer service and Customer Relationship Management..

As your sphere of influence expands, the things that, previously, you could only register a concern over become smaller as they morph into what you can influence. Take environmental change as an example. You might believe global warming is only something you can be concerned about because you are limited in your ability to do anything about it. "It is beyond my pay grade" is the often-quoted response in the corporate world. However, if you make the decision to recycle, reduce your carbon footprint, or switch to solar energy, you are influencing the impact of global warming on our planet. You can expand your influence by controlling who you vote for (something you can control in most countries); through your vote, you influence laws and policies. If you choose to become an activist, your influence on the issues that concern you expands even further. While the final decision may be "beyond your pay grade", taking action on what you can control can influence the final decision. Just like the marathon which seems difficult and may be even impossible after your first practice run, environmental change can become something you can control and influence. It is indeed *not* beyond your pay grade. It is only beyond your pay grade if you choose not to move.

Of course, it is often difficult to know *how* to move when there is so much you don't know. And even what you know can change. To make the right moves – to take action that is productive and effective – try reframing your thinking (see the chapter on Perspective) along these lines: "Knowing what I know and also knowing what I don't know, what are my choices?"

Welsh consultant Dave Snowden, author of *The Cynefin Model*, spent a great deal of time pondering the same question[4]. Using *Cynefin*, the Welsh word for habitat or place, Snowden created a framework to try to make sense of the place we find ourselves in. The framework consists of five scenarios:

Complex: Where there are unknown unknowns; there are too many unrelated dots or undiscovered dots to be connected. For example, the beginning of the COVID pandemic.

Suggested action: **Hypothesize, experiment, deduce.** Make no regret moves. Fail fast (not fatally) and move on. The answer will present itself after a few experiments.

Complicated: Where the action and the outcome may depend on a series of facts and actions. We know the unknowns. Different sets of facts have to be analyzed and there will be dots to be connected. For example, most consumer behaviour in retail.

Suggested action: Engage with experts to **research (find the unknowns) and analyze** before formulating a response.

Chaotic: Where the cause and effect are too confusing and much is unclear and unknown. Knowns become unknowns. New unknowns emerge.

Suggestion action: **An action is always better than no action.** For example, first responders' reaction to a burning building: get everyone out of harm's way first even if the cause of the fire and how severe it is or will become is unknown.

Clear/Obvious: Where an action is known to or is likely to lead to a known outcome.

Known facts, known risks; even known unknowns. If I did this, I know that will happen (or will very likely happen). For example, a system or process breakdown or repairing or upgrading a machine.

Suggested action: Adopt **best practices** based on what worked in the past.

The fifth scenario is "CONFUSION" where the situation is an evolving combination of any or all of the above. Indeed, it is not even clear which scenario is at play.

In this state of affairs, Snowden suggests approaching the whole situation in parts. Indeed, the modus operandi when there is confusion should be "observe (fast), compartmentalize, and move", then, very importantly, repeat. In order words, confusion is a continuum. Even if you think you have put out the fire, be ready, in the chaos of the situation, to put out another one and possibly with a different method. Each step should be aimed at reducing the confusion and moving into one of the above other four scenarios, at least into chaotic, if not into complex.

Using MYPRISM to develop an action plan

This takes us back to where we started: using MYPRISM as the foundation of your action plan; applying these principles as you contemplate what action you need to take:

1. M – mindfulness, internal and external
2. Y – why/purpose/objectives
3. P – perspective/observation
4. R – reality/validation
5. I – inquiry/inspiration
6. S – staging/laying out your options, readying your resources
7. M – move – execute on your plan.

After you have contemplated MYPRISM, start designing your action plan by first creating SMART goals[5]. SMART stands for *Specific, Measurable, Achievable, Relevant,* and *Timely.* In Chapter 7, we discussed extensively how you should stage out your options, including being clear about determining the resources you would need (including their level of competency) and how you would deploy them. Each action that you lay out to achieve your SMART goal should be grounded on your purpose "Why" - hence the need for a "relevant" goal. If not relevant, scrap it.

A way of being, a mindset: overriding your autopilot

For some people, exercising is not a chore. They just go to the gym or cycle or jog or swim regularly. No complaints, no resistance. For others, exercise is an often-dreaded activity that must be done. The key lies in habitualization. If you approach MYPRISM as a checklist of things that you *have* to do in order to overcome your autopilot, you are setting yourself for resistance. Instead, make MYPRISM your habit. If you approach every situation with MYPRISM in mind, over time this approach becomes your way of being.

Mindfulness, like meditation, improves with practice. The first time you try meditation, it is likely you will fall asleep. Keep working at becoming mindful. Eventually, you can stay mindfully alert, even when silently meditating, without falling asleep.

While some people are naturally born athletes, we can all be athletes if only we form the habit of healthy living. Healthy living is not automatic. It takes practice. It becomes a habit. Once it is a habit, it sticks with minimal depletion.

Practicing MYPRISM should not be depleting. If everything you do is a matter of your purpose, your perspective, your inquiries, your staging, and your moves will always be mindful and purposeful. MYPRISM will be less of a checklist and more of how you operate. It will be less of a chore and more something you are intrinsically motivated to accomplish.

MYPRISM starts with mindfulness, for how you think becomes who you are. Rather than let your actions be your legacy, let your mind determine your destiny. Mahatma Gandhi famously said:

Your beliefs become your thoughts,
Your thoughts become your words,
Your words become your actions,
Your actions become your habits,
Your habits become your values,
Your values become your destiny.

Your autopilot is not always grounded by your values. It is mostly your default reaction based on anxiety and past practices. Unless you flip the paradigm, your actions may take you further and further from your values and only towards your fears. Don't let your fears be your destiny. Instead, unleash your creativity for your best self to come forth.

After you put this book down, we hope you start your next move in MYPRISM. Otherwise, this will just be another book you have read. There will be no change from your autopilot.

Key take-aways from this chapter

1. Awareness and insights do not matter if there is no action. You need to *move*.

2. Moving or changing is hard; we normally resist moving unless there is tension for learning.

3. Tension need not be borne from fear and anxiety. Ground your action on creativity instead.

4. Let your brain experience the joy of success first before overwhelming it with the stress of the tasks at hand.

5. In our VUCA world, there are more reasons to fear and be anxious.

6. Different situations require a different approach to action.

7. Hone your skills to recognize the situation you are being confronted with and learn to be comfortable making decisions.

8. Practice, practice, practice.

Your new autopilot is yet to be discovered.

CHAPTER 9

CASE STUDY and EXERCISE

Throughout this book, we used coaching stories with characters like Florence, Amnezza, Mike, Donna, Derrick, and Alex to illustrate the principles behind MYPRISM. To honour and protect the privacy of all our clients, we have deliberately disguised the characteristics of the characters and their circumstances. The names are all fictional. The coaching principles and outcomes are, however, based on real situations.

The following case study is based on a composite of actual executive coaching done by the authors. We created this case study both as a recap of the principles behind our approach in MYPRISM as well as to demonstrate that the practice of MYPRISM is not sequential. While it is anchored in mindfulness, it does not follow that "Y" comes next and before "P" (perspective) and then "R" (reality) and so forth. MYPRISM is about a new way of approaching crises, to disrupt and turn off your "autopilot", to face reality for what it is, and to find the most effective, impactful solution forward. For it to work, all of MYPRISM may be fired simultaneously or in some cases only certain elements of MYPRISM are required. In other cases, more or less weight is placed on one element than the next. We hope to use this last case study to demonstrate this. We inserted some exercises for you to practice MYPRISM. You can use these exercises to launch your practice of MYPRISM. Have fun!

Famada started their day as on any other day, with ten minutes of guided meditation. They clicked on the APP on their mobile phone and followed the soft quiet voice of the mediation guru for the next ten minutes. This day, however, felt different. They were not able to quiet their mind. Something was dominating their mindshare. While they were very aware of their environment and have reflected on it, they were not able to "focus". Checking on their Cs, they rated themselves low on "Calm". Why might this have been the case? What else was going on? What might have increased their "calm"?

Without labelling, they were already doing one of the I's: Inquiry. What was going on at work, at home? Well, it was the upcoming project that was about to be announced – the CEO would be announcing a major acquisition on a global scale. As the head of products in North America, Famada would be charged with integrating product development and product manufacturing across regions. In some cases, products would be duplicative, and in other cases they would be complementary. There would be so many decisions. There would be so many tense meetings. *"So much change and so many unknowns ahead. How can anyone expect to be calm?"*, Famada thought to themself. Let's see if you can try to help Famada.

Exercise 1: Going back to mindfulness and C for calm, what can Famada do to elevate their calm? How can "P" for perspective help?
Your Thoughts Here:

_____

_____

_____

_____

In this case, simply being clear on their questions helped Famada realize that many of their questions were based on assumptions and coloured by their previous experience of a hostile acquisition. The same may not necessarily apply for this impending merger. So, what might bring clarity to the situation? What are the realities in this transaction? What data would Famada need to feel better about the things to come? Who can be a counterpart who might share a different perspective?

Exercise 2: What questions (inquiries) would you encourage Famada to ask about the impending deal?

Your Thoughts Here:

_____

_____

_____

_____

_____

During a coaching session with one of the Kantologos, we first worked on Famada's anxieties: the need to be a decisive and effective leader and a good advisor to the CEO. Do they need to know all the answers to fulfil this role? What are the CEO's expectations? What else is going on besides work that is fuelling this need to be decisive and a good advisor? What happens if Famada is not a good advisor to the CEO?

These questions help Famada better understand the "Y" of their situation. Famada has risen in the corporate ranks by being the hard charger to drive sales through organic growth. It is beyond dispute amongst their peers that Famada was the top person for developing a top selling product year after year. The acquisition would be the first time that growth for the company would be achieved without Famada's direct contribution. Famada was coached to acknowledge this anxiety. They accepted that this anxiety might be clouding their perception of what the reality meant for themselves as well as for the company. Upon understanding that their anxious brain was in high gear, Famada was invited to return to their mindful meditation. How would this anxious brain be allowed to calm down and step back? After a few meditation sessions, Famada was able to see a creative pathway to face the impending acquisition.

Exercise 3: How do you think Famada switched their perspective which in turn guided their inquiries and staging for the next step?
Your Thoughts Here:

_____

_____

_____

_____

Famada identified a Senior Vice President from the M&A team who was able to brief them on the *raison d'être* of the deal. What was the strategic value of the acquisition to the company and what were assumptions about what this acquisition would mean in terms of accelerating growth? Famada then set up time to talk to their boss, the CEO, and they agreed on the role that Famada might play in the coming transaction and how Famada might help the company launch a new chapter of growth. Famada was immediately energized. After the meeting, and despite the excitement and a clear understanding of the expectations the CEO had of them, Famada became anxious again. They understood the power of "inquiry" but the more they did that, the more they came to the conclusion that they knew very little of how to integrate the two businesses. Inquiry did not help so far. More meditation? The reality was beginning to look more and more complicated and therefore more stressful.

In the next coaching session, Famada was encouraged to reflect on MYPRISM. Which part of the PRISM can be the most help to re-activate their creative brain and to calm their anxious brain? How would Famada inspire their team to support them in carrying out their role to realize the aspiration of the company? What more data does Famada need and where can they find that? Might the team know things that Famada did not? Might the team have a different perspective (P)? Can their team help them know what else they don't know but will be able to navigate despite the incomplete data? Famada was invited to come up with a "staging" (S) plan – what can be done, what must be done now? What can be done post-merger? What needs to be done after the merger, in which sequence? How can the plan change or flex?

Exercise 4: If you had to draft Famada's staging plan, what might it look like? Your plan should include steps that would inspire the team to embrace the new reality – that the company will be bigger and more global.

Your Thoughts Here:

_____

_____

_____

In developing their staging plan, Famada was very deliberate on assumptions and on known facts of their own company and the acquired business. The drafting of the staging plan required more perspective-taking and reality checking. Assumptions seemed less "scary" now because Famada's team were all-in and raring to go. The team felt inspired (I) and everyone was motivated to come up with the best ideas despite the many unanswered questions in this early stage of the deal. Making assumptions in fact unleashed more creative thinking. But hang on, Famada suddenly felt perhaps they are getting ahead of themselves. Could there be wishful thinking where a realistic execution plan was needed? Well, how can Famada be sure of their reality (R)? What can Famada do to achieve a high level of confidence that the staging (S) was executable vs. a pipe dream? *"Shouldn't we just wait and see?"*, Famada thought cautiously.

Exercise 5: Can you think of any reason why Famada might be hesitant to take the first steps towards the new reality? What might be gained or lost if Famada took some steps now? What might be gained or lost if Famada did nothing until the acquired business had been legally transferred? Which of these "staging" activities would bring Famada closer to their goal of being a trusted advisor to the CEO and an inspiring leader for their current team and their new team?

Your Thoughts Here:

In their next coaching session, Famada was invited to reflect on the last element of MYPRISM – M for move. What might be causing the inertia to act? Famada considered the perspective of the CEO as well as the perspectives of their team. They in fact took a further step: to view the transaction from the perspective of the business that was going to be acquired. A whole different set of inquiries and investigations took hold. With the guidance of their legal team, mostly through the use of a "M&A clean room", Famada was able to start conversations with their counterpart prior to the legal closing of the merger. Working on their own mindfulness, focusing on the reality of the present and a new set of inquiries, Famada started to see "reality" through the lens of the other party. The staging plan now took into account the resources and capabilities of the other team as well. Famada no longer felt the pressure of going it alone. In fact, they proactively set a cadence with the senior leadership team to review the merger integration plan. Each month, the entire team reviewed the changing circumstances, asked questions, checked each other's assumptions and committed to making decisions to move the plan along. In the process, Famada was able to live their role as the trusted advisor both to the CEO and their peers.

Recently, we checked in with Famada. They reiterated their routine of starting the day with guided meditation. On some days, Famada didn't even need to tab on the APP on their mobile phone. Famada was able to sit with their thoughts and arrive at clarity for the tasks for the day – starting with who they needed to be for the moment, for the team, for themself. It is not always 10 out of 10 mindfulness of course. There will always be moments of uncertainties since the world is constantly changing.

The speed and frequency of change in Famada's business world are "real". This can be a source of depletion. The unknown and the untested will also be scary. However, Famada was able to take the perspective that the same source of anxiety can equally be a source of inquiry and staging. Acknowledging the "Y" in any situation helped Famada tap more into their creative brain. Any move that Famada makes is now less burdened by the worry that it is finite and an ending in itself. Rather, it is a move that will lead to more inquiries, more staging and more checking in with reality and demands of the moment.

Famada's autopilot to jump in and take immediate action is now frequently switched to the "off" position and replaced by the practice of MYPRISM; that is their new way of arriving at a purposeful response to any situation.

Epilogue

"You must be joking" was one of the more polite comments we have heard when mentioning to our friends and colleagues that the six of us were going to write a book together. And it is true: usually books are written by one person, sometimes two authors collaborate; and if you are a celebrity, then the book cover mentions your name and adds "written with so and so", indicating that the other person has done all the heavy lifting while your name sells the book. Then there is, of course, the authoritative handbook on whatever the theme might be that has been edited by a few people based on many individual contributions, which is more a collection of contributions than one book. The format of our endeavour is therefore rather unusual. In a way, the sheer fact that you can read this book now is proof that autopilot can be switched off, more perspectives can be found, collaboration and friendship can be forged, and great things can happen when the courage, curiosity, and energy triumvirate join forces.

We are the Kantologos and we shared the heavy lifting and the joy of writing MYPRISM. Everyone engaged in ideating, writing, reading, editing, and cheering each other on, challenging one another, and creating good energy during our exclusively virtual meetings, spanning six locations across seven time zones. It is true that this book would never have seen the light of day without the pandemic and the shift in work and collaboration patterns that resulted. We would never have gotten to know one another had it not been for Carol Kauffman's splendid idea of asking for volunteers from the group of Fellows of the Institute of Coaching to talk more deeply about *Resilience*. The six of us serendipitously heeded the call. We showed-up and stayed throughout the journey. The rest, as they say, is history and described in the introduction to this book.

We certainly have many people to thank and acknowledge. We dedicate this book to all our families, friends, and loved ones as well as our mentors, clients who inspired us, encouraged us, and sustained us through this journey. We are also grateful to all fellow coaches from whom we have learned and future coaches to come who we hope to inspire. We also want to use this epilogue to reflect on what we have learned while writing this book.

It is a lot easier to create an idea than to give birth to the actual product. During ideation, it is easy to get carried away by the excitement of an idea or the enthusiasm of your friends and colleagues, and not to see all the legwork and the heavy lifting needed to articulate the idea into words in a cogent structure. The creative process was in itself the best testament to MYPRISM at work. We checked our mindfulness of our internal conditions and mutual external goals. Why do we even want to write this book? What is our purpose? We asked many questions that challenged each other's perspectives. And then we asked more questions, prompting each other to read this and research that. We asked even more questions, all the time focusing on how we might inspire our readers. In each step, we reminded ourselves of our realities and the reality of getting a book published, let alone encouraging anyone to buy and read it. We had to stage our deliverables and track our progress and hold each other and ourselves accountable and finally move towards a printable book.

The group has helped each of us get around several hurdles, including the familiar one of sitting in front of a blank piece of paper or screen for too long. Our conversations about the ideas have been so rich that there was always a place from where to begin to get a few ideas down. Soon, we created a structured approach, like a skeleton onto which we then added more detail. Then we were able to assign ourselves roles and responsibilities. We followed through for the Kantologos.

So, what did we learn along this creative process? That diversity in thought definitely results in a more enriched and enlightened outcome. That a team of many is always going to outperform a team of one. Research and more research are good, but you need to MOVE from a baseline and start writing. That the first step is the hardest but if you don't even do that, you will never get anywhere. One step (one word on a piece of scrap-paper) is infinitely more than zero. When you feel a bit lost, go back to your original purpose. Check and re-check your reality – as your reality changes (client meetings, coaching calls, family demands, health, etc. etc.). That we are all part of a system. We are never really a lone wolf having to struggle alone – no matter our inclinations. Many forces are in our favour. We just need to see them, believe in them, and tap them. The result emerges, like magic, without depletion (well, some exhaustion, but always exhilarating).

Unsurprisingly, the time, energy, and dedication needed for moving from seven raw pieces of writing to one consistent book are enormous. Progress seems to be slow, wordsmithing takes time, and it is easy to forget that a change in one chapter might have repercussions throughout the entire book. Again, MYPRISM came to our rescue. We literally practiced what we were writing, which in turn strengthened our conviction that this book has great potential to have a good and meaningful impact. It is way more than a compendium of essays and thoughts.

In writing as in life, our different personalities, strengths, preferences, and focus areas come through, and different qualities are needed across different phases of the project. At the same time, it is fantastic to know that any individual shortcoming will be covered by someone else's strength. Bonded by our collective purpose and friendships, we trusted the process and each other. We all felt psychologically safe in each other's company. Dissent is not criticism, dissent is an obligation. Dissent is an invitation for us to think harder and be more creative. It results in the better version of what we produced and how we evolve as coaches and as individuals.

We are very grateful for this book, for what it did to us, can do for us, and very importantly to all our readers. We are immensely grateful to each other.

Finally, thank you, dear reader, for the time you spent with MYPRISM. We hope MYPRISM will help you see your autopilot and that while your autopilot has helped you in the past, it is not your only way forward. We hope that you develop the ability and courage to switch off your autopilot and let MYPRISM reveal more viable solutions to move forward that are close to your values and purpose. Knowing the steps of MYPRISM will anchor you when or if uncertainty and disruption knock you off balance.

Go to: www.Kantologos.com to join the conversation.

Notes

Chapter 1

1. https://www.alumni.hbs.edu/events/Pages/crisis-management.aspx.

2. Jamais Cascio, "Facing the Age of Chaos," Medium, April 29, 2020, https://medium.com/@cascio/facing-the-age-of-chaos-b00687b1f51d.

3. Jamais Cascio, "Facing the Age of Chaos," Medium.

4. Bob Johansen, *Leaders Make the Future: Ten New Leadership Skills for an Uncertain World.* (Oakland: Berrett-Koehler Publishers, 2012).

Chapter 2

1. Fernando Pessoa, *The Complete Works of Alberto Caeiro.* (New York, NY: New Directions, 2020).

2. "Mindfulness," Psychology Today, https://www.psychologytoday.com/us/basics/mindfulness.

3. Susan David, Ph.D., author of #1 Wall Street Journal Bestseller, *Emotional Agility* (New York, NY: Avery, 2016), is one of the world's leading management thinkers and an award-winning Harvard Medical School psychologist.

4. Jon Kabat-Zinn, *Wherever You Go, There You Are: Mindfulness Meditation in Everyday Life.* (New York, NY: Hachette, 2005).

5. Dan Goleman and Richard Davidson, *Altered Traits: Science Reveals How Meditation Changes Your Mind, Brain, and Body.* (New York, NY: Avery 2017).

6. Maria Gonzalez, *Mindful Leadership: The 9 Ways to Self-Awareness, Transforming Yourself and Inspiring Others.* (San Francisco, CA: Jossey-Bass, 2012).

7. Janice Marturano, *Finding the Space to Lead.* (London: Bloomsbury Press 2014).

8. Chade Meng Tan, *Search Inside Yourself: The Unexpected Path to Achieving Success, Happiness (and World Peace).* (San Francisco, CA: HarperOne, 2014).

9. Clif Smith, *Mindfulness without the bells and beads.* (New York, NY: Wiley, 2021).

10. Daniel J. Siegel, *Aware: The Science and Practice of Presence.* (New York, NY: TarcherPerigee, 2018).

11. "Awareness," Wikipedia. Accessed on Nov. 13, 2022. https://en.wikipedia.org/wiki/Awareness.

12. Daniel J. Siegel, *Aware.*

13. Siegel, *Aware.*

14. Siegel, *Aware.*

15. Daniel Goleman, "The Focused Leader," *Harvard Business Review,* December 2013.

16. Goleman, "Focused Leader," 2013.

17. Goleman, "Focused Leader," 2013.

18. Kantologos (Aleman, M., Choo, D., Lazar, J., Masterman, B., Morais, F., Pfeiffer, R.), "Compendium on Resilience" (2021).

19. See, for example, Jacqueline Brassey et al., *Deliberate Calm: How to Learn and Lead in a Volatile World.* (New York, NY: HarperBusiness 2022).

20. T.S. Eliot, *The Four Quartets.* (New York, NY: Ecco, 2023).

21. Donald A. Schön, *The Reflective Practitioner: How Professionals Think In Action.* (Milton Park: Routledge, 1984); and Donald A. Schön, *Educating the Reflective Practitioner: Toward a New Design for Teaching and*

Learning in the Professions (San Francisco, CA: Jossey-Bass, 1991).

Chapter 3

1. Ventral pallidum (VP), see these findings by Stephenson-Jones et al., published in the article, ""Opposing Contributions of GABAergic and Glutamatergic Ventral Pallidal Neurons to Motivational Behaviors," Neuron (2020), https://pubmed.ncbi.nlm.nih.gov/31948733/.

2. The Gestalt School of thought (founded in 1912, Germany) emphasizes the human brain's approach to context and structure. We respond to individual items differently depending on context. The same singular word would mean different things when used with other words in a different context. Hence, the need for the human brain to work find structure and closures from all inputs.

3. See, for example, Richard Ryan and Edward Deci, *Self-Determination Theory: Basic Psychological Needs in Motivation, Development, and Wellness.* (New York, NY: Guilford Press 2018).

4. Deci and Ryan labelled this form of motivation as "Introjection" – an internalized extrinsic motivation.

5. Deci and Ryan labelled this as "Identification".

6. D. E. Berlyne, "A theory of human curiosity," *British Journal of Psychology,* 45, (1954).

7. Recall the Steven Covey quote, "We see the world, not as it is, but as we are."

8. Freud, "Repetition Compulsion."

9. Thorndike's Law of Effect.

10. For example, Kylie Rochford, Scott Taylor etc.

11. Richard Boyatzis, "Leadership development from a complexity perspective," in *Handbook of Managerial Behavior and Occupational Health.* (Cheltenham, UK: Elgar, 2009).

12. Richard Boyatzis and Annie McKee, *Resonant Leadership: Renewing Yourself and Connecting with Others through Mindfulness, Hope, and Compassion* (Boston, MA: Harvard Business School Press, 2005).

13. Richard C. Schwartz and Martha Sweezy, *Internal Family Systems Therapy* (2nd edition). (New York, NY: The Guildford Press, 2019).

14. 2019 Coaching client of View Advisors LLC with identity withheld and modified.

Chapter 4

1. These instinctive reactions involve the choice between fight, flight, and freeze – although the threats faced by our ancestors, thousands of years before us, are vastly different from the threats we face today. For most of us, the usual threat does not come in the form of a saber-toothed tiger anymore, triggering the "will you be lunch for me or will I be lunch for you" ultimatum. As a result, the reaction to unexpectedly seeing a saber-toothed tiger may not be appropriate as part of our standard repertoire any longer (unless, of course, if we are somewhere in the wilderness where even lesser species than a saber-toothed tiger might be a real danger).

2. Lisa Feldman Barrett is a distinguished professor of psychology at Northeastern University and - at the time of first publishing this book - author of two books:, *How Emotions Are Made:* The Secret Life of the Brain (Boston, MA: Mariner Books, 2017) and *Seven and a Half Lessons about the Brain* (New York, NY: Picador imprint of MacMillan, 2017).

3. See, for example, Richard Boston and Karen Ellis, *Upgrade: Building Your Capacity for Complexity,* (Bristol: LeaderSpace, 2019) for the section on perspective, different points of view (positions or types of perspective) that can be taken, as a way of getting better at understanding other people's worlds.

4. Essentially, Daniel Kahneman argues that we spend most of our time in what he refers to as System 1, a fast, automatic, emotional, and intuitive way of dealing with our reality, leading to the use of habits allowing for intuitive problem-solving; only after considerable effort, we switch on what he refers to as System 2, a slow, deliberate, and rational way of using our cognition to take in and weigh information and come to informed conclusions and actions.

5. In 2006, David Rock interviewed UCLA-based neurobiologist Jeffrey Schwartz about how the brain functions (Rock, 2006). Schwartz, citing a 1983 study of voluntary movement by Libet, notes that once the brain sends us an urge to act a half-second before we register it consciously. Our actions are preceded by that urge by 0.3 seconds. The control we had over voluntary movement only became available in the last two-tenths of a second before we moved. "It seems we may not have much 'free will' but we do seem to have

'free won't' – the ability to not follow our urges."

6. We first heard this question asked at a retreat in 2017 put on by Alan Seale, founder of the Center for Transformational Presence.

7. Conscious "being" is a form of "inner doing". It is self-leadership in action.

8. Douglas Choo, "A leader's resilience: Not as intuitive as you think", LinkedIn, June 17, 2020, https://bit.ly/3K23yQ8.

9. Ronald A. Heifetz and Marty Lensky, "A survival guide for leaders," *Harvard Business Review* (June 2002).

10. Among them Manfred Kets de Vries and Friedemann Schulz von Thun.

11. Heffernan, Margaret. *Wilful Blindness: Why we ignore the obvious at our peril.* (London, UK: Simon & Schuster, 2011)

12. Richard C. Schwartz and Martha Sweezy, *Internal Family Systems Therapy* (2nd edition). (New York, NY: The Guildford Press, 2019).

13. See, for example, Amy Edmondson, *The Fearless Organization: Creating Psychological Safety in the Workplace for Learning, Innovation, and Growth,* (New York, NY: Wiley, 2018), and T.R. Clark, *The Four Stages of Psychological Safety: Defining the Path to Inclusion and Innovation,* (Oakland: Berrett-Koehler, 2020) for how psychological safety can be developed in groups that will allow contribution and challenge.

Chapter Five

1. Under optimal conditions, requests for coaching reflect a desire to further build strengths. However, the usual circumstance and trigger is a recognized gap between current and desired behaviour. This often involves strengthening behaviours that interfere with desired performance. Her manager saw a developmental opportunity. The senior leadership team may have been more concerned with following and documenting legal procedures for addressing substandard performance.

2. Rewire Inc. "How to overcome cognitive biases and make better decisions." Medium. November 21, 2017. https://medium.com/swlh/how-to-overcome-cognitive-biases-and-make-better-decisions-daeecd38f910

3. Marshall Goldsmith. *What Got You Here Won't Get You There: How Successful People Become Even More Successful.* (London: Profile Books, 2008)

4. Barry Johnson. *Polarity Management: Identifying and Managing Unsolvable Problems.* 2nd Edition. (Pelham, Mass: HRD Press, 2014).

5. John Lazar & William Bergquist. "Alignment Coaching: The Missing Element of Business Coaching." *International Journal of Coaching Organizations.* 2003, 1-1, 14-27. https://researchportal.coachingfederation.org/Document/Pdf/2905.pdf

6. Fred Kofman. *Conscious Business: How to Build Value through Values.* (Louisville, CO: Sounds True Publishing, 2013)

7. Aaron Hurst. *The Purpose Economy: How Your Desire for Impact, Personal Growth, and Community is Changing the World.* (Boise, ID: Elevate Publishing, 2014).

8. Edgar H Schein. *Organizational Culture and Leadership.* 5th Edition. (San Francisco, CA: Jossey-Bass/Wiley, 2016).

9. Schein. *Organizational Culture and Leadership*

10. Amy C. Edmondson. *The Fearless Organization: Creating Psychological Safety in the Workplace for Learning, Innovation, and Growth.* (Hoboken, NJ: Wiley, 2018).

11. Julia Rozovsky . "The Five Keys to a Successful Google Team." ReWork. November 17, 2015. https://rework. withgoogle.com/blog/five-keys-to-a-successful-google-team/

12. Amy C. Edmondson. *Teaming: How Organizations Learn, Innovate, and Compete in the Knowledge Economy.* (San Francisco, CA: Jossey-Bass/Wiley, 2012).

13. Carol S. Dweck. *Mindset: The New Psychology of Success.* (New York, NY: Ballantine Books, 2007).

14. Daniel Goleman. *Emotional Intelligence: Why It Can Matter More than IQ.* (New York, NY: Bantam Books/ Random House, 2005).

15. For the value of this framing, see Susan J. Ashford. *The Power of Flexing.* (New York, NY: Harper, 2021).

16. David J. Snowden & Mary E. Boone. "A Leader's Framework for Decision Making." *Harvard Business Review.* November, 2007. https://hbr.org/2007/11/a-leaders-framework-for-decision-making

17. One of the opportunities afforded by experimentation was for Derrick to consider different possible realities, beyond what he had initially considered. This led to discussions, thought partnership with his coach,

and analysis of the wider range of options now under consideration.

18. Edmondson, *Teaming.*

19. Richard Boston & Karen Ellis. *Upgrade: Building Your Capacity for Complexity.* (London, UK: LeaderSpace, 2019).

Chapter Six

1. Leonard J. Marcus, Eric J. McNulty, Joseph M. Henderson, Barry C. Dorn. You're It: Crisis, Change,and How to Lead When It Matters Most. (New York, NY: PublicAffairs, 2021).

2. Celeste Kidd and Benjamin Hayden, "The psychology and neuroscience of curiosity" *Neuron.* 2015 Nov 4; 88(3): 449-460.

3. Jennifer Brown. *How to be an Inclusive Leader: Creating Trust, Cooperation, and Community across Differences.* (Oakland, CA: Berrett-Koehler Publishers. 2019).

4. Merriam-Webster online https://www.merriam-webster.com/ dictionary/integrate

5. Brian Christian & Tom Griffiths. *Algorithms to Live By: The Computer Science of Human Decisions* (New York, NY: Henry Holt & Co/Macmillan, 2016).

6. The same could be said for any strong emotion. Is the audience angry? Sad? Defiant?

7. Marcus et al, You're It

8. Todd Kashdan, David Disabato, Fallon Goodman, Carl Naughton. "The Five Dimensions of Curiosity". *Harvard Business Review,* September - October 2018. https://hbr.org/2018/09/the-five-dimensions-of-curiosity.

9. Claudio Fernández-Aráoz, Andrew Roscoe, Kentaro Aramaki. "From Curious to Competent". *Harvard Business Review,* September-October 2018. https://hbr.org/2018/09/from-curious-to-competent.

Chapter Seven

1. Steven R. Covey. *The 7 Habits of Highly Effective People: Restoring the Character Ethic.* (New York, NY: Free Press/Simon & Schuster, 2004).

2. Kali Shulklapper. "Jane Fonda Didn't Start the Fire – But She's Putting It Out". *Chief.* January 29, 2021. https://chief.co.uk/articles/jane-fonda.

3. Amy C. Edmondson. *The Fearless Organization: Creating Psychological Safety in the Workplace for Learning, Innovation, and Growth.* (Hoboken, NJ: Wiley, 2018).

4. Adam Grant. *Think again: The power of knowing what you don't know.* (New York, NY: Viking/Penguin Random House, 2021).

5. Adam Grant. *Think Again.*

6. Chip Heath and Dan Heath *Made to Stick: Why some ideas take hold and others come unstuck.* (London, UK: Arrow Books/Penguin Random House, 2008).

Chapter Eight

1. Albert Bandura. *Self-efficacy: The exercise of control.* (New York, NY: W.H. Freeman/Times Books/ Henry Holt & Co, 1997).

2. Steven R. Covey. *The 7 Habits of Highly Effective People: Restoring the Character Ethic.* (New York, NY: Free Press/Simon & Schuster, 2004).

3. Steven R Covey, *7 Habits.*

4. David J. Snowden. "Cynefin, A Sense of Time and Place: An Ecological Approach to Sense Making and Learning in Formal and Informal Communities". *ResearchGate.* 2011. https://www.researchgate. net/publication/264884267_Cynefin_A_Sense_of_ Time_and_Place_an_Ecological_Approach_to_Sense_ Making_and_Learning_in_Formal_and_Informal_ Communities.

5. George T. Doran. "There's a S.M.A.R.T. way to write management's goals and objectives". Management Review, November 1981. https://community.mis. temple.edu/mis0855002fall2015/files/2015/10/ S.M.A.R.T-Way-Management-Review.pdf.

Bibliography

Bibliography

Ashford, Susan J. *The Power of Flexing*. New York, NY: Harper, 2021.

Bandura, Albert. *Self-efficacy: The exercise of control*. New York, NY: W.H. Freeman/Times Books/ Henry Holt & Co, 1997.

Barrett, Lisa Feldman. *How Emotions Are Made: The Secret Life of the Brain*. Boston, MA: Mariner Books, 2017.

Barrett, Lisa Feldman. *Seven and a Half Lessons about the Brain*. New York, NY: Picador/MacMillan, 2017.

Berger, Jennifer and Catherine Fitzgerald. "Coaching for an Increasingly Complex World: Principles and Practice." Accessed December 20 2021. https://bit.ly/3x8hSyR.

Berlyne, D. E. "A theory of human curiosity." *British Journal of Psychology,* 45 (1954).

Boston, Richard, and Karen Ellis. *Upgrade: Building Your Capacity for Complexity*. Bristol: LeaderSpace, 2019.

Botelho, Elena Lytkina, Kim Rosenkoetter Powell, Stephen Kincaid, and Dina Wang. "What Sets Successful CEOs Apart: The Four Essential Behaviours That Help Them Win the Top Job and Thrive Once They Get It." *Harvard Business Review*. May–June 2017.

Boyatzis, Richard. "Leadership development from a complexity perspective." *Handbook of Managerial Behavior and Occupational Health*. Cheltenham, UK: Elgar, 2009.

Boyatzis, Richard, and Annie McKee. *Resonant Leadership: Renewing Yourself and Connecting with Others through Mindfulness, Hope, and Compassion*. Boston, MA: Harvard Business School Press, 2005.

Brassey, Jacqueline, et al. *Deliberate Calm: How to Learn and Lead in a Volatile World.* New York, NY: HarperBusiness, 2022.

Brown, Jennifer. *How to be an Inclusive Leader: Creating Trust, Cooperation, and Community across Differences.* Oakland, CA: Berrett-Koehler Publishers. 2019.

Cascio, Jamais. "Facing the Age of Chaos." *Medium.* April 29, 2020. https://medium.com/@cascio/facing- the-age-of-chaos-b00687b1f51d.

Choo, Douglas. "A leader's resilience: Not as intuitive as you think." LinkedIn. June 17, 2020. https://bit. ly/3K23yQ8.

Christian, Brian, and Tom Griffiths. *Algorithms to Live By: The Computer Science of Human Decisions.* New York, NY: Henry Holt & Co/Macmillan, 2016.

Clark, T.R. *The Four Stages of Psychological Safety: Defining the Path to Inclusion and Innovation.* Oakland: Berrett-Koehler, 2020.

Conant, Douglas R. "The Power of Idealistic-Realism: How Great Leaders Inspire and Transform." HBR.org. January 12, 2012. https://hbr.org/2012/01/the-power-of-idealistic-realis.

Covey, Steven R. *The 7 Habits of Highly Effective People: Restoring the Character Ethic.* New York, NY: Free Press/ Simon & Schuster, 2004.

David, Susan, Ph.D. *Emotional Agility.* New York, NY: Avery, 2016.

Doran, George T. "There's a S.M.A.R.T. way to write management's goals and objectives." *Management Review.* November 1981. https://community.mis. temple.edu/

mis0855002fall2015/files/2015/10/S.M.A.R.T-Way-Management-Review.pdf.

Dweck, Carol S. *Mindset: The New Psychology of Success.* New York, NY: Ballantine Books, 2007.

Eaton, Paul D., Antonio M. Taguba and Steven M. Anderson. "The military must prepare now for a 2024 insurrection." *Washington Post.* Accessed December 17, 2021. https://wapo.st/3DYgYsu.

Edmondson, Amy. *The Fearless Organization: Creating Psychological Safety in the Workplace for Learning, Innovation, and Growth.* New York, NY: Wiley, 2018.

Edmondson, Amy C. *Teaming: How Organizations Learn, Innovate, and Compete in the Knowledge Economy.* San Francisco, CA: Jossey-Bass/Wiley, 2012.

Einhorn, Cheryl Strauss. "11 Myths about Decision-Making." HBR.org. April 11, 2021. https://hbr.org/2021/04/11-myths-about-decision-making.

Eliot, T.S. *The Four Quartets.* New York, NY: Ecco, 2023.

Fernández-Aráoz, Claudio, and Andrew Roscoe, Kentaro Aramaki. "From Curious to Competent." *Harvard Business Review,* September-October 2018. https://hbr.org/2018/09/from-curious-to-competent.

Forbes. "The World's Most Valuable Brands." Accessed June 27, 2021. https://www.forbes.com/powerful-brands/list/

Fox, Lior, Ohad Dan, Lotem Elber-Dorozko, and Yonatan Loewenstein. "Exploration: from machines to humans." *Current Opinion in Behavioural Sciences.* 2020, 35:104-111.

Goffee, Robert, and Gareth Jones. "Why Should Anyone Be Led by You?" *Harvard Business Review.* September–October 2000.

Goldsmith, Marshall. *What Got You Here Won't Get You There: How Successful People Become Even More Successful.* London: Profile Books, 2008.

Goleman, Daniel. *Emotional Intelligence: Why It Can Matter More than IQ.* New York, NY: Bantam Books/ Random House, 2005.

Goleman, Daniel, "The Focused Leader." *Harvard Business Review,* December 2013.

Goleman, Daniel, and Richard Davidson. *Altered Traits: Science Reveals How Meditation Changes Your Mind, Brain, and Body.* New York, NY: Avery 2017.

Gonzalez, Maria. *Mindful Leadership: The 9 Ways to Self-Awareness, Transforming Yourself, and Inspiring Others.* San Francisco, CA: Jossey-Bass, 2012.

Grant, Adam. *Think again: The power of knowing what you don't know.* New York, NY: Viking/Penguin Random House, 2021.

Hagel, III, John. "Good Leadership is about Asking Good Questions." HBR.org. January 8, 2021. https://hbr.org/2021/01/good-leadership-is-about-asking-good-questions.

Harvard Business School. https://www.alumni.hbs.edu/events/Pages/crisis-management.aspx.

Heath, Chip, and Dan Heath. *Made to Stick: Why some ideas take hold and others come unstuck.* London, UK: Arrow Books/Penguin Random House, 2008.

Heifetz, Ronald A., and Marty Lensky. "A survival guide for leaders." *Harvard Business Review*. June 2002.

Hurst, Aaron. *The Purpose Economy: How Your Desire for Impact, Personal Growth, and Community is Changing the World*. Boise, ID: Elevate Publishing, 2014.

Johansen, Bob. *Leaders Make the Future: Ten New Leadership Skills for an Uncertain World*. Oakland: Berrett-Koehler Publishers, 2012.

Johnson, Barry. *Polarity Management: Identifying and Managing Unsolvable Problems*. 2nd Edition. Pelham, Mass: HRD Press, 2014.

Kabat-Zinn, Jon. *Wherever You Go, There You Are: Mindfulness Meditation in Everyday Life*. New York, NY: Hachette, 2005.

Kantologos (Aleman, M., Choo, D., Lazar, J., Masterman, B., Morais, F., Pfeiffer, R.). "Compendium on Resilience." 2021.

Kashdan, Todd, and David Disabato, Fallon Goodman, Carl Naughton. "The Five Dimensions of Curiosity." *Harvard Business Review,* September - October 2018. https:// hbr. org/2018/09/the-five-dimensions-of-curiosity.

Katsos, John E., and Jason Miklian. "A New Crisis Playbook for an Uncertain World." HBR.org. November 17, 2021. https://hbr.org/2021/11/a-new-crisis-playbook-for-an-uncertain-world

Kidd, Celeste, and Benjamin Hayden. "The psychology and neuroscience of curiosity." *Neuron.* 2015; 88(3): 449–460.

Kofman, Fred. *Conscious Business: How to Build Value through Values*. Louisville, CO: Sounds True Publishing, 2013.

Lazar, John and William Bergquist. "Alignment Coaching: The Missing Element of Business Coaching." *International Journal of Coaching Organizations.* 2003, 1-1, 14-27. https://researchportal.coachingfederation. org/ Document/Pdf/2905.pdf.

Marcus, Leonard J., and Eric J. McNulty, Joseph M. Henderson, Barry C. Dorn. *You're It: Crisis, Change, and How to Lead When It Matters Most.* New York, NY: PublicAffairs, 2021.

Marturano, Janice. *Finding the Space to Lead.* London, UK: Bloomsbury Press 2014.

McNulty, Eric J. "The CEO Can't Afford to Panic." HBR Case Study. March 1, 2010.

Merriam-Webster online. https://www.merriam- webster. com/ dictionary/integrate.

Pessoa, Fernando. *The Complete Works of Alberto Caeiro.* New York, NY: New Directions, 2020.

Psychology Today. "Mindfulness." https://www. psychologytoday.com/us/basics/mindfulness.

Rewire Inc. "How to overcome cognitive biases and make better decisions." *Medium.* November 21, 2017. https:// medium.com/swlh/how-to-overcome- cognitive-biases-and-make-better-decisions- daeecd38f910.

Rozovsky, Julia. "The Five Keys to a Successful Google Team." *ReWork.* November 17, 2015. https://rework. withgoogle.com/blog/five-keys-to-a-successful- google-team/.

Ryan, Richard, and Edward Deci. *Self-Determination Theory: Basic Psychological Needs in Motivation, Development, and Wellness.* New York, NY: Guilford Press, 2018.

Schein, Edgar H. *Organizational Culture and Leadership.* 5th Edition. San Francisco, CA: Jossey-Bass/Wiley, 2016.

Schön, Donald A. *Educating the Reflective Practitioner: Toward a New Design for Teaching and Learning in the Professions.* San Francisco, CA: Jossey-Bass, 1991.

Schön, Donald A. *The Reflective Practitioner: How Professionals Think In Action.* Milton Park: Routledge, 1984.

Schwartz, Richard C., and Martha Sweezy. *Internal Family Systems Therapy.* 2nd edition. New York, NY: The Guildford Press, 2019.

Shulklapper, Kali. "Jane Fonda Didn't Start the Fire — But She's Putting It Out." *Chief.* January 29, 2021. https://chief.co.uk/articles/jane-fonda.

Siegel, Daniel J. *Aware: The Science and Practice of Presence.* New York, NY: TarcherPerigee, 2018.

Smith, Clif. *Mindfulness without the bells and beads.* New York, NY: Wiley, 2021.

Snowden, David J. "Cynefin, A Sense of Time and Place: An Ecological Approach to Sense Making and Learning in Formal and Informal Communities." *ResearchGate.* 2011. https://www.researchgate. net/publication/264884267_Cynefin_A_Sense_of_Time_and_Place_an_Ecological_Approach_to_Sense_Making_and_Learning_in_Formal_and_Informal_ Communities.

Snowden, David J., and Mary E. Boone. "A Leader's Framework for Decision Making." *Harvard Business Review.* November 2007. https://hbr.org/2007/11/a-leaders-framework-for-decision-making.

Stephenson-Jones, Marcus, et al., "Opposing Contributions of GABAergic and Glutamatergic Ventral Pallidal Neurons to Motivational Behaviors." *Neuron.* 2020. https://pubmed.ncbi.nlm.nih.gov/31948733/.

Szumowska, Ewa, and Arie Kruglanski. "Curiosity as end and means." *Current Opinion in Behavioural Sciences.* 2020, 35:35-39.

Tan, Chade Meng. *Search Inside Yourself: The Unexpected Path to Achieving Success, Happiness (and World Peace.* San Francisco, CA: HarperOne, 2014.

Toomer, Jerry, and Craig Caldwell, Steve Weitzenkorn, and Chelsea Clark. *The Catalyst Effect: 12 Skills and Behaviours to Boost Your Impact and Elevate Team Performance.* Bingley, UK: Emerald Publishing, 2018.

Wikipedia "Awareness." Accessed Nov. 13, 2022. https://en.wikipedia.org/wiki/Awareness.

Index

Figure 6.1. The 3 I's of Inquiry, 111
Figure 6.2. The Iceberg, 121

A
action plan, 11, 155
Aleman, Maribel P., 5
Algorithms to Live By, 125
Amanda, 113–17
Amnezza, 42, 47–49, 61
Annual General Meeting (2021), 5
anxious brain, 52, 57, 149–50, 163–64
assumptions, 13, 30, 33, 78, 91, 94, 97–102, 105, 110, 161, 163, 165–66

B
behavioural choices, 6, 43, 47–51, 62
behavioural science, 12
biases, 13, 74, 76, 85, 91, 93–95, 105, 121–22
Brown, Jennifer, 122

C
Cascio, Jamais, 8–9
Choo, Douglas, 5
cognitive skills, 12, 15, 18, 44, 46–47, 52, 56, 149
context, 13–14, 21, 28, 72, 88–89, 91, 96, 100, 103, 105, 111
Corporate Leadership Development Program, 24
Covey, Stephen, 152
COVID-19, 8, 120
Crisis Management for Leaders, 8
culture/psychological safety, 101

D
dark side of autopilot, 11
data, 13–14, 89, 91–92, 96–97, 118–19, 122, 126–27,

132–34, 136, 162, 164
David, Susan, 21—22
Deci, Edward, 49—50
Derrick, 90, 92—104, 160
Donna, 88—89, 104—106, 120

E
Edmondson, AC, 104
elements of MYPRISM, 160, 166
emotional intelligence, 24, 27
emotional reaction, 15, 30, 44, 152
emotional self-regulation, 103
emotional stimulus, 56
epistemic curiosity, 52
"epistemology of practice," 38
Ernst & Young Mindful Leadership Program, 24
extrinsic motivations, 50–51, 62

F
"Facing the Age of Chaos," 8
Famada, 160–67
Feedback, 360-degree, 82—83
filters, 76–79, 82, 85
five Cs, 30–31, 161
Florence, 18–20, 160

G
Goleman, Dan, 22, 27
Gonzalez, Maria, 23–24
Google, 23–24, 102
growth mindset, 103

H

How to be an Inclusive Leader, 122

I

inquisitive mind, 27
instinctive reactions, 66
Institute For The Future (IFTF), 8–9
Institute of Coaching. See IOC
intercultural dimensions, 81
intrinsic motivation, 50, 62
IOC (Institute of Coaching), 4, 66, 170

J

James, LeBron, 72, 119–21
Johansen, Robert, 9

K

Kabat-Zinn, 22
Kahneman, Daniel, 68
Kantologos group, 4
Kauffman, Carol, 4, 8, 70, 170

L

Lazar, John B., 5
leadership practices, 23, 116
leadership skills, 126–27

M

Map of Objects of Awareness and Focus, 27–28, 38
marathon, 138, 150–51, 153
Mary (pseudonym), 58–60
Masterman, Beth, 5
metaphor of a Prism, 10–11

Mike, 64, 79, 132–34, 137–40, 142–44, 160
mindful leaders, 24–25, 33–35, 37–38
mindful leadership, 23, 27, 37–38
mindful meditation, 163
Mindfulness-Based Stress Reduction (MBSR), 22
monocultures, 44
Morais, Fernando, 5
Mumbai, 82
MYPRISM in action, 15

O
Oliver, 113–16

P
perspective-taking, 68–69, 72, 76, 80, 165
Pfeiffer, Rolf, 1
Point of view, 64–65, 82, 105
practice of MYPRISM, 116, 123, 160, 167
priorities, 21, 74, 80, 96, 102, 135
prismatic leaders, 112, 129
psychological safety, 102, 104, 139–40, 145
psychometric assessments, 49
purpose, 6, 12, 14, 25–26, 42, 44–48, 101, 133, 137, 152, 155–56, 171, 173

R
"reflection-in-action," 37
Refraction, 10–11
Ryan, Richard, 49—50

S
scenarios, 44, 74, 148, 154–55
Schwartz, Richard, 76

Search Inside Yourself (SIY), 23–24
self-compassion, 58
self-leadership, 34
Siegel, Daniel J., 25–26
skilled leaders, 110, 122, 124, 127–29
Snowden, Dave, 153–54
solar energy, 153
source of anxiety, 167
source of depletion, 167
source of empowerment, 43
source of inquiry, 167
source of motivation, 49–50, 150
source of validation, 50
sources of stress, 60
stress hormones, 43

T
"Taking perspective," 67
Thinking Fast, Thinking Slow, 68
Tokyo, 82
Tversky, Amos, 68

U
unconscious biases, 13, 76–77
US East Coast, 82

V
values, 30, 33, 36, 42, 48–51, 59, 61–62, 74, 80–81,
101–2, 111, 144–45, 157
Victor, 113–14
VP Human Resources, 92
VUCA world, 9–10, 12, 15, 18, 150, 157

W

"Wheel of Awareness," 26

Y

Yeni, 132–33, 135, 138, 141–42

Z

Zhou, Zhuang, 53

CPSIA information can be obtained
at www.ICGtesting.com
Printed in the USA
LVHW031439020523
745888LV00016B/912/J